EMOTIONS, FEELINGS, AND UNDERSTANDING ONE'S SELF!

By: Jerry W. Miller

I have been wanting to write about emotions for sometime now. You may ask just what my credentials are to undertake such a topic. I have been taught by the most important teacher of all times, in the most revealing classroom ever to exist. I have been taught by the experiences of life, the way it has touched my heart and soul through the experiences of making my way through its tragedies and thus finding within my soul insights that could only have touched me by experiencing life's full emotional spectrum.

I, like you, have wondered just what my emotions are? Why do I feel the way I do at times? Why can't I feel happy all the time?

Am I a victim of my emotions? Must I ride a roller coaster of feelings having no control over them? Both tragedy and ecstasy have a way of making us reach into our inner being and there and only there can we find any answers.

To begin, we are not slaves to our emotions. We are trained in many facets of our lives, but no one has really taught us how to handle and work with our emotions. It seems to be a subject that is too forbidden to share with each other, or even to understand or study within our own self.

I feel we have done others and ourselves a great injustice by hiding our emotions, clouding a beautiful part of us that should be open and exciting. Perhaps by allowing ourselves to truly experience and interact with our emotions and those of others on a true plain, many of the hurts of this world would not emerge.

We spend our whole lives in search of many things, following like sheep those around us that perceive life's value is in the many things we have, the designer clothes, the nice cars,

EMOTIONS, FEELINGS, AND UNDERSTANDING ONE'S SELF!

Copyright May 15, 2026
By: Jerry W. Miller

PREFACE

Writing about emotions in this day and age of suppressed and subdued emotions was no easy task, especially in this never before seen era of 'Social Distancing!' We all experience our own perception of emotions and their stimulation and guidance both passively and actively on our lives. We find emotions a factor within ourselves that we hide because we have never been taught that our emotions and feelings are a sacred part of our make up and are to be cherished, not hidden from view.

It appears that our world is settling into a cold essence of being, stifling our emotions. We need to counter this by giving our emotions value, by listening to them, letting them guide us into a stronger spiritual relationship within ourselves and our counter parts.

We must **live** our emotions. We must allow others to live out theirs' also. We must encourage a more sensitive sense of being, centering our essence, and freeing our soul to truly let life touch it with the complete spectrum of emotions that are necessary for us to experience a full value of life here before moving onto the next.

Since emotions are such a closed subject, but one that we all experience and wish to share, I suggest while reading this you set aside some of your quiet time for yourself. Find somewhere that you can relax without being disturbed, and gently reflect upon this book while reading it, letting it touch and stir your own emotions.

homes, all the tangible items that we cherish so much. Nowhere along the line do we store a savings account of our emotions, our feelings. Nowhere do we share ourselves with each other for fear of dissipation of our values, ridicule, or alienation from our peers.

True, there are many emotional thieves in this world. Many people will attach to anyone with a strong personality, one that displays a grace within their being, a sense of realization that they are content with themselves, that they perhaps love themselves.

Sometimes one attaches to another out of desperation because they feel that they can indeed fill a void within themselves by absorbing qualities from another, thus making them a more whole being. You cannot take these values from another being in anyway. The life you perceive here is much different than anything that you can imagine. We are here to learn about life from this plain of existence. We have to learn to love ourselves first, then others, and to help each other lovingly while in life's boundaries.

It is so simple to explain the why that we are, the why we exist, but most people complicate their lives and souls with many reasons, denials, fallacies, for they are searching for themselves on the wrong level within this plain of life.

Most things in this life do not matter. We need sustenance. We are material beings in a material world; therefore we need material items in order to feel a part of this awareness. We can make ourselves feel physically comfortable within this realm, and that is part of our way of maintaining the illusion of existence here. But once we complete this primary bout of physical enhancement, once we are physically set within our life bond, then we must search farther. We must search our soul, our intellect, and our very essence for other answers that are far more important than those that we have answered for the physical. If you denied the physical completely, you would die. All our ancestors and for that matter all of us will die from this view of life eventually.

Life is just a view of consciousness on this level. It matters not how successful you are in your physical attributes of life. You must reach your plateau of comfortability that will bring you to the level of realization that you must seek elsewhere for your growth. You must turn your soul away from wherever you are and reach forward. It is this step, this realization of the other parts of you that will manifest and enhance your soul to new goals, new inner realizations of reason, of intellect, intelligence, and awareness.

You must realize that you are a wonderful and wondrous being, far higher on the chain of life than you imagine. You must come to the realization that you are a finite part of a wonderful plan of a Supreme Being that is allowing you an enhancement awareness of a field of view that is such a delicate and intricate part of existence that it is beyond your comprehension, even when you are walking within its boundaries. You must realize that you are given the intellect, the knowledge, the sensitivity to be fully aware of all of life's secrets, of the over all plan of your being and your place in that plan.

Sometimes it seems that it takes a slap in the face, so to speak, to open people's realization, mind, and emotions in order for them to step outside of their own bounds and take a dramatic look at their essence and their interplay with the life and reality they are so a part of. It seems that one must befall great harms in life, be they physical, emotional, or conditional before one turns their essence outwards.

It is only by looking away from one's rationale; one's reality, one's valued set of logic, place in life, for you to reach an apparent awareness that will allow the expansion of your being.

If you question yourself as to why tragedy has befallen you, no matter what it might have been, you must reach your soul back through your complete journey of life. You must realize that everything that has happened to you, every piece of love, hurt, anxiety, empathy, every experience be it emotional, physical, or spiritual, all combined makes up the you that you conceive yourself this day.

You must also realize that there is and never will be another being like yourself, that you are unique to yourself, those around you, and the universe. If any of the hurts that had befallen you, or for that matter any of the other experiences you experienced had not happened, and you had not been affected by those experiences, you would not be the unique and beautiful person you are this day.

You must realize this uniqueness of yourself, this grandeur of your being. Once you do, you will know the importance of experiencing all facets of life, all emotions, everything that can possibly affect you in any way. It is this interplay with our reality that is our reason for existing momentarily on this plain of life.

To not interact, to not experience any and all of these values would make our three dimensional experience a two dimensional bore and we might as well be cut out dolls being moved around a precious, but non meaning world, existing only of a flat surface of valueless and meaningless experiences.

As I look back at my life, I am happy that everything that happened to me, both good and bad, happened just the way it did, for I am happy with myself. I truly love myself. If all the good experiences, all the hurts, the tragedies, all combined allowed my essence to be as it is at this moment, then I am thankful that all that did happen, happened to me and I would not change any part of it.

True, my life has not been a rose bed of physical, emotional, or intellectual experiences, but if all together, they instilled within me the values I have in intellect, emotions, empathy, and spirituality then they all had a positive meaning on my soul and life.

Though our recorded past exists unchanged and is as it will forever be, we are not bound to its linear continuation be it physical, intellectual, or spiritual. We are beings of great powers over our existence. We create more of our life than we will ever be aware of. The person you are that exists in this very moment is a culmination of all the facets of your wanting to be your own special person up to this point.

Our destiny is not left in the hands of anyone else. We have control over ourselves and it is this control that has brought us to the point of existence we are this very day. You may want to rationalize against this premise. You may truly convince yourself otherwise, but if you reflect deep within your soul you will realize that life is a series of choices and it was your choices that eventually led you down life's path to the point of reflection that you are today.

Many of us try to blame everything else for our own failures, our hurts, and our woes. It is much easier to pass this responsibility for our own shortcomings on to another figure, any figure other than our own selves. We spend much too much of our time doing this, letting our life flow meaninglessly, waiting for someone or something to give it direction. Many of us spend our complete lives **wandering** instead of **searching** for our happiness and our growth.

Our emotions are ours to command. We are not at their mercy. Sure, we react emotionally to certain stimuli, mainly because that is an inbred pattern either by instinct or learned response. We are not slaves to these responses. We can take control of our emotional interaction with our surroundings and our environment. We are in charge!

We must question any value of our make up that seems to stagnate our development. We must learn from our experiences and analytically intermingle our feelings and our logic in a way that neither runs rampant with our essence.

It is hard to say that we should logically plot our emotions because we feel that logic and emotional values are of two non-bending plains of our make up. This is not so! Sure we can logically dispel our feelings of love, of emotional inter-play with our counterparts, but we can use the logic within our souls to dispel any unwarranted feelings or emotions that are of such a negative value that they impede our journey in development.

There is a difference between learning from a negative experience in life and creating many more negative experiences needlessly. We are to be touched lightly by life, not beat into emotional submission by it.

In this life we teach others how to treat us and likewise with our own emotions. If you continue on a self-pity pattern of existence, you will set up powerful forces to create this end.   If you must chart your life by negativities, they will manifest and cage you in both mind and soul.

Life is a linear cosmic awareness of one's soul and a playground to test and enhance one's being. You are a physical being in a physical world, but this world this essence of yourself is but an illusion, an awareness that will soon dissipate once you leave through the door of our conceptual rationale called death. Once you journey back to creation and change your awareness towards another plain of life, the values you enhanced your soul with will not only be a part of your real self, but also be its very make up.

The thoughts you think, the feelings you feel, the values you partake in, the wants, the hopes, the aspirations, the love, and the emotions, all these are the real you. Upon death your body will be released and your attention will no longer have this plain of reality to validate itself. The factors that you have learned are now the reality you are becoming. You are what you felt, and thought, and cherished. The only values that you will take with you through death's door are the memories, the emotions, the empathy, the intellect, the hopes, the fears, and the love that you created as your experience here in this life.

The awareness that we are now is not the totality you might think it is. The you that you feel is you is but a small part of yourself. Your awareness in this plain is minute to the total you that really exists. You are at your own mercy and no one else's. You can change any and all values of self no matter what they might be. You are only a conceptual value of the 'direct being' that you allow as your appearance in this dimension we call life.

You will continue to play the role you are this day, this life, till you reach back into your soul and change your 'direct beings' interplay with this reality. You can change this experience as you wish, but **you** must take control, **you** must be the one to decide on the conscious and 'direct conscious' levels which direction to chart your soul.

Any and all emotions must be experienced. Emotions and thoughts are tangible items. They exist as sure as anything physical exists on this earth. We try to deny this. We chart life with our logic and make many things seem illogical so we can rationalize and discount what truths we are afraid to face about ourselves.

The truth is that logic really does not exist in the over all plain of existence. It is just a set of rules that we determine as a working guideline to our world and life with in a variable time frame that is fluctuating and changing the values of its own identity at each intellectual step with in our perceptions. Logic values are as transient as the illusion of time; neither have validity except for the fact that we want them to identify an inner craving for continuing our identity factions.

We must experience and learn from our emotions. We must validate them. If we deny them they will return to us many times over. They will be masked in many ways and we will have to either face or wear that mask until we recognize and accept or deal with those emotions.

We as humans seem to only validate those things within our culture that physically affect us. These physical items are only perceptual, conceptual, stimulations that we have chosen to affect our being in such a way as to make us counter them on their plain, and force our awareness away from ourselves outwardly into other dimensions of existence and growth.

Emotions are one of our most valued assets. They are the key that our Creator has given us to open many doors of our being. Be thankful that you can experience the complete spectrum of emotions, for if you lacked any of them you would be unable to grow or enhance while within the experience of life.

If you only experienced a few emotions, your idea of reality would become tainted and likewise your soul, for you would not correctly view life as it was meant to be. You would be stifled in your ability to enhance your identity and expand yourself and your revelations to your counterparts in the true identity you are so illusionary and illusive to while here.

Your life here is a mask of your true identity. It is such a small part of your true self, but unlike a mask, as we know them, it changes the wearer behind the mask.   The more experience you attain in this mask, the truer image of your soul is changed or molded to the identity you are formulating here. The mask is not a one-way vehicle of change though. You can change it with the intellectual and emotional stimuli you receive from life, or you can change your life by re-imaging your 'direct self.'

When I refer to your 'direct self', I am referring to the reality, the true totality of your being, the inner being, and the soul that is you, but has not woven itself into the totality of this reality. The 'you' that you conceive, is but a small fragment of this 'direct self.' It is this 'direct self' that is your true reality and most people do not become aware of this concept while living within life's bounds.

This is why most things that befall us really do not individually matter. All these experiences, though we wish them to all be good, are part of an enhanced learning experience that exists only because our 'direct self' is allowing us to maintain this illusion of life. This illusion lasts only for the time it takes our 'direct self' or 'direct awareness' to receive its concept of a full value experience of this plain, then it redirects its awareness elsewhere.

The sharing bond you have with others continues but in a much different way than you could possibly conceive. The concepts we perceive as our reality and our total existence are only tangible and comprehensible to our image while we exist here. True life doesn't abide by these rules or concepts because they are imaginary and illusive. They were conceived for us to have a like experience in this plain only, and exist only to give us guidelines to this dream we are in awareness of.

The idea of ownership of existence is a fallacy. We are sharing creatures of a higher level of life. We are one within ourselves, but also a part of the overall essence of a multitude of higher existences that are of such a wonderful culmination of experiences that we are unable to conceive their true identity. This is because we are so fixed upon our reality that we seldom let our minds and souls wander back to the awareness of our 'direct selves' where in lies all the answers not only to this mask of life, but the direct sharing of all knowledge be it intellectual, emotional, or spiritual.

Every experience ever created, shared, or woven into existence by any soul in effect is shared by every other soul to ever have existed, for life is a shared experience. We are now and have never been alone within our world of existence.

Loneliness or Solitude

Loneliness is a perception that has no validity other than the fact that you have turned yourself momentarily from your true awareness of self. You have reached your essence outward blindly trying to capture a value, a feeling from someone else, rather than creating it within your own being. You have sought life from another's experiences and have not tried to 'share' your essence with others.

Loneliness is a choice, not a condition. It may be hard for you to accept the fact that you choose to be lonely, but it is a fact. There are literally billons of people on this earth, and if you as one individual can not find company from any one of that multitude of souls, then you have turned your essence from all those around you only by choice. You may rationalize many reasons as to why you are lonely, but you are only fooling yourself.

You must not confuse loneliness with solitude. You must be able to be alone with yourself and relish in the experience, for your best and most trusted friend must be your own soul. You must learn to be alone and love yourself, for then and only then can you develop, understand, and direct this value towards others.

Fear of loneliness causes much strife in our lives. Many people destroy their lives because of it, or settle themselves into an existence that is either superficial or meaningless. If you are afraid to be alone with yourself, then you can do nothing short of emotionally draining those that you surround yourself with.

Loneliness is a way of your soul telling you that you are viewing life only outwardly with your peers. You are not reflecting within yourself and growing emotionally and spiritually. It is much too easy to float emotionally down the stream of life depending on others to make you special, make you seem important even to ones' own self. It shows that you have lost control and contact with your identity and must have validation of your worth by others for your life to have meaning.

It is this lack of control of one's life, this relentless passive attitude towards your make up that eventually segregates your will from your soul. You create your loneliness because you can only feel a true part of all existence when you yourself **love** yourself!

If you seek all life elsewhere, you will only find the scraps from another's table of life. You must create concrete evidence of life's values within your own soul. Then and only then can you share your essence, your life, and your love with others. You must put no more love in another soul than you have put in your own. You cannot give forth anything in this life that is not a part of yourself.

Love must come from within; it is not a borrowed quality. You must have the inner feelings of peace within your soul. You must come to the realization that it is your self-love, your inner love that starts the flicker of light that manifests itself outward warming other souls as you touch them in your life.

You may bask in the light and warmth of an others' love, but when they turn their love elsewhere, and at some point in their existence and yours, they will, even if it is at the point of death, you will find yourself in a darkened environment of emotions, for the light was only a reflection from your soul, warming it momentarily. Once their warmth is distinguished, there is nothing within your own being to create its own haven of enlightened repose.

Self-Love

Self-love is not vanity. Vanity is loving one's flesh and personal or physical belongings. Self-love is just understanding how life has touched you, and no matter how wonderful or harmful, learning from that experience by reaching into your soul and enhancing your awareness of your place in this life and those to come. It is acknowledging that you are a wonderful being. You are special to yourself, your peers, and your creator and you have learned of love and life, of all kinds of emotions, and you have been seasoned but not hardened by them.

Self-love is the only validation that one can place upon their existence. All else fades as we turn from this life to another. The only thing that we take across the void to other plains of life is the love we show and share this and every day.

By coming into acceptance of one's self, one can then show empathetic cause and reasoning for those around them. If one realizes that on the larger spectrum of life that everything we do directly effects the whole consortium of existence, and that what ever emotions or feelings you display to your counterparts here on earth, you are also affecting your own existence, for we are one entity.

Empathy

I feel the emotion empathy is next in line to love in our makeup. In a way it is the ultimate mode for loving others. To me empathy is reaching into another's soul and not only understanding their feelings, their hurts, and their emotions, but also helping them to cope with those negative things that they are dealing with. This is accomplished by pointing them towards the door that will lead them to a more comfortable way in their plight!

We can in no way experience another person's life, but we can help to lighten another's burdens. We must realize that the feelings that touch us, the hurts that seem unbearable have been experienced in some form, some way by others. Just as we can learn to do anything else in life, there are tried and true ways to help us to deal with these emotions.

We were never taught that we aren't slaves to our emotions. Many of us wander down life's paths for years suffering needlessly because we feel we have no control over our emotions and the way we feel. When a dark cloud over shadows us, it is hard to see the sunshine on the other side of it. We feel we must ride through the storm and let it stop our soul at its' will until it moves on by its' own accord.

This is not so! We have control over our emotions. We want to think that all of our emotions are an outward cosmic effect that programs our lives. We resort to the horoscope, numerology, the occult, anything that will allow us the freedom from having to take control and charge of our own emotions, life, and soul.

We can raise our spirits, our thoughts, our emotions, and our lives above the storm if we but take control of our emotions. Passivity is a slow form of death when it comes to one's feelings and emotions. Many of us want someone else to take control of our lives, to give us advice, to tell us how to react or interact in our relationships with others, and even ourselves. Few people have control of their own lives or emotions. They spend so much energy compiling, sorting, creating, enhancing, and depleting their own values of life's comments upon their souls. Just think then, how can they also take control of yours and lead you to emotional safety?

There are certain mechanics of how emotions and feelings affect us, how we interact with them, perceive them, relish in them, and change them. You sometimes can be given insight into how to deal with your emotions and feelings by others, but they cannot reach inside your soul and feel for you. They cannot take control of or direct your emotions, feelings, or soul.

You are the only one that has control over these things. Of course, others can direct forms of control over you. They can enslave you in many ways, but no one can enslave the essence of your soul. You and only you can relinquish that part of yourself. If you ever do this or have ever done so, you can reverse the effect by just realizing that **you** are in control over your own essence, your emotions, and your identity on this plain of life and your destiny.

Aggression

Aggression is but a person's unclear mark on their existence. It is a bi-fold concept that can only exist because there is a counter part that is willing to relinquish their identity to another. Aggressors, no matter to what degree, are reaching out to suppress another's values for they are trying to subdue feelings in themselves that they can not comprehend or create with in their own being. They are trying to steal a value that they lack and feel is necessary to make them complete and whole within themselves.

Insecurity

Insecurity is an interesting emotion, because all of us experience it to some degree. Most people have an inner feeling of insecurity of their relationships, their jobs, or themselves in some degree. To deny this is to lie to one's self. There has never been a soul walk this earth that at one or more times has not questioned their own validity, premise, and reasons for continuation of being.

Insecurity, like most other emotions, is unique in its own way. It is so rampart, so a part of everyone, and so denied by most who posses it. It is the one emotion that has no facts to establish its validity.

I believe that insecurity is just another word for comparison. We compare our lives with others, usually those that appear to have more than we do. More tangible items is the first premise; more friends, more relationships, a stronger personality, better looks, anything and everything that we can use to deny the basic fact that we are no higher or no lower on life's scale than anyone else. Our plateau in this life is of our own making.

If we must use comparison to allow validation, why must we compare our lesser values? Why not resort to comparing our like values or our positive assets? We are inbred with the choice of choosing negatives first. We go out of our way to seek out negativity, to expose it, and to prove its worth to ourselves and those around us. We have been brought up with the word 'no' and have integrated its negative premise into our make up as a basic building block of our emotional character.

We create our being more than you will ever conceive. We are not left to the winds of life to blow our soul in whatever direction the emotional weather forecast predicts at a given moment.

Our lives are not predestined because the stars happened to be in a certain correlation to each other the moment we were born from the womb according to the horoscope. The absurdity of our self-validation factors astounds me. We relinquish our control over our existence by almost anything, even to giving over our destiny to a note in a fortune cookie!

This is because we have never been taught that we are such great creators. Our destiny, our life's value on this earth is not predetermined, not pre-programmed, or not left to the whims of anyone else. We allow various values in our society to overshadow this truth.

Our true make up is a very complex thing. If you reach into your soul you will find amazing insights and a revelation into the true meaning of your being. Your quest for learning from life, love, and your intellectual drive are your reasons for viewing life's gallery here.

Collectables

You must collect many things in this life, for your journey here was just for that purpose. I speak not of the tangible items that we seek so dearly most of our lives, those are left behind. I speak rather of the emotional values we conceive and mold our pre-existence with. The love, the hopes, the aspirations, the denials, the empathy, the caring, the sharing, the euphoric spiritualistic resonation of our souls while we are within life's boundaries, our thoughts, our remembered emotions, our love, are the collectibles that we are here to seek and find.

If we live our lives in a two dimensional, non-emotional effect, then we will be short handed when we return to our true essence, our true direct being, and our life's journey will have been of little meaning. It is the essence of our well being of soul that we must partake in, enhance, and accredit our soul with as something supreme to carry an essence of love back with us to add to the overall perception of life.

Greed & Selfishness

Greed and selfishness exist only during your perception of animated life in this dimension. All energy, all thoughts, feelings are a combined and shared effect. It is only your inner mistaken perception that fools you into thinking otherwise. The items that you cherish as your own, the greed you aspire in is a momentary joke that you are portraying upon yourself. You own nothing but the identity marker that is your soul, your single cell of essence faction of the overall interim effect of life.

If you aspire to greed and selfishness within this life you are but only causing yourself to direct your awareness away from the valued sharing of the direct self and quarantining your values   momentarily   from   your   own comprehension allowing your treasures to be shared by all but yourself.

Hate and Negativity

Hate is an emotion that is the most destructive of all! It destroys the fabric of spiritual harmony of the creator, putting a wall between themselves and all the balance of their life. It is the supreme negative experience one can enter into while here within life's boundaries.

Hate takes more energy from its creator than any other emotion. It drains it in direct proportion to the intensity one perceives their hatred. Hate directed at another is a tear within one's soul and only by letting it go can one rise above and conquer it. Hate is an emotion that can only be sustained by the one doing the hating, and it is not worth the effort or the energy.

I concede that within our journey down life's paths we encounter entities, ideals, concepts, and burdens that tear into our soul. We with all our might want to hate them away from our existence. We have all experienced this and will continue to experience this in some from and to some degree. We must not let this emotion build up within our being to such intensity that it destroys our very life's fabric and eats away at our essence.

You must protect yourself from certain things in life, certain forces, and certain people that have violated their rights for conscious continuum on your level. You must not let them draw you emotionally into a web of deceit that your soul will adhere to with such intensity that you are drawn emotionally and intellectually into a dimension of negativity. That will turn your view from this earthly plain and make up of life being that of love, loving one's self, others, and enhancing one's essence spiritually, physically, and emotionally to a darker side of existence that you will forever regret!

Forgive and Forget

It is best to forgive and forget those that have transpired against you and your soul. Anything less will just give them a bond, a continual hold over you. This is not to say that you should with all your mind, heart, and soul try to make amends if your distancing from them was something you might have inadvertently caused.

Tyranny

When someone directs negativity towards you in whatever form, it is because of a lacking they have in their own entity, their make up, their emotional being, and their very soul. The tyrants of the world are the saddest lot. They are the totality of insecurity within their own little worlds and must make validation of their conceptual selves by trying to subdue other's hearts, souls, minds, and make up.

Tyranny must be stood up to at all costs. You must not be led by anyone else into paths that your inner being says is not right. You must learn your rights, and respect, and expect them for yourself and those around you. You must aid others in their plight if they are less sure of themselves. By reaching out your hand and pulling them along in life to a better stature is also helping you to enhance your own soul.

Prejudice

The Price We Pay For Embracing our Prejudices!

We seem to take solace and comfort by embracing the Prejudices we have amassed in our journey through life. They are a product of, or influenced by our place of birth, religious affiliation, current local or global events, time frame in history we came into being, or exposure from our family, friends, media, or our church. We learn to hold them close to our bosom, heart, mind, and very soul as though they are more than just an influence on our being, but the very fabric of the make up of our mind, body, and soul.

We are sometimes slowly talked into various prejudices by those same forces from our family, friends, churches, news media, or political parties. We create a safe 'Tribal' mental and sometimes physical wall around ourselves so we can safely feel comfortable within the various prejudices that we have woven into our fabric of being, mind, and soul. It is as though we are often times drawn to different prejudicial righteousness from the 'Tribe' or 'Group' or 'Family' or 'Organization' that will validate our prejudices. They can make them seem palatable to not only our lives, but also our beliefs in this world and the one that may come after our life experience here. That is if you believe in an afterlife.

By surrounding ourselves by any one of these entities, lets call them 'Tribes' for lack of anything more definitive, we validate, justify, and make peace within our mind, body, soul, and our form of God and the hereafter that any of the prejudices we embrace are heaven sent.

We can then justify our inner hatred, abhorrence, dislike, disgust, revulsion, or repulsion towards another person, race, religious affiliation, sex, sexual orientation, color, intellectual level, position on the financial ladder, or political party of anyone that is not a part of our particular 'Tribe!' Therefore 'They' are not of the 'Chosen' and

'Acceptable' and 'Graced by God' as 'We' have come to believe that 'We' and the other members of our particular Tribe are.

We don't really realize just what an enormous price we pay for embracing our prejudices! It is far from that of just walling our individual selves and our 'Tribe' off physically from others. It also prevents us from becoming aware of the beautiful things we could learn, be a part of, accept, create, and transform not only our lives but also the world in general with from others that are not part of our closely knit Tribe! It winds up blocking our minds, bodies, and souls from the beauty that we cannot see through the filtering prisms of our prejudices that we hold up not only in front of our eyes, but our very souls.

If you look at any baby, fresh from the womb, you will find a complete loving, intriguing, happy, embracing, forgiving, tolerating, inquisitive, and wide eyed wonder of a young soul. You will see him or her looking out at not only its mother and father, but from that birthing moment forward, on outward to its family, its neighborhood, its schools, its town or city, its State, and its country.   This continues on and on to the many concepts it will eventually be made aware of and embrace. These will eventually include the universe and his or her place in it and their destiny in our world setting their paths forward be they righteous or devious.   They will all be unheeded, uninhibited, and unspoiled to begin with - simply pure, concise, and innocent at that first moment of birth and life.

From that beautiful little being's birth, its destiny is created, formed, manipulated, guided, and molded by all the things that it is exposed to. The most influential of all is the little prejudices its parents, doctors, teachers, surroundings, peers, religious and political leaders, and the interaction with other 'Tribes' instill in it as it matures its way into life.

A baby cannot become prejudice in any way shape or form without the influence and exposure of another person's or 'Tribes' various forms of prejudice. One of the toughest prices we pay for embracing our own prejudices is to pass them on to our children or peers or friends or family or 'Tribe.' By doing this, not only are we paying the price for embracing our prejudices, but our children and their children for many generations may well be paying the price for our prejudices also! Because the prejudices we wear as either a badge of honor, or a shield of protection, or a cross of self-purity that we decided was God's will, they become not a prejudicial trait in our minds, but a blessing of purity to those we pass them on to. We then believe that they will somehow open heaven's gates for members of our 'Tribe' only and not of those we bare our cross of prejudices against.

Prejudices come in the form of many negative things that we just don't think about or realize! Some of us wear them like an ancient Roman Gladiator's shield to protect us from that 'evil' we perceive of another person or race or religion. Some of us wear them as a 'banner of being a better person' than those that we are prejudice against. The most misguided are those that wear their prejudices as either a Holy Cross or God blessed banner exalting only them above everyone else and therefore making them closer to God than those they feel are of a lesser character or moral fiber than themselves.

Your prejudices may sometimes feel like a warm blanket wrapped around you on a cold day! They surround you and shield you. They make you feel safe, sound, and warmed to the very core of your mind, heart, and soul! You cannot believe your prejudices are anything other than a heaven sent blessing upon you and that you are righteous and blessed to be comforted by them.

We all need to look into a mirror and reach deep into our souls and confess our prejudices to our peers, our God (if we believe in one), and ourselves! This will give us a reality check into our true beliefs and perspectives of our lives and those we interact with at all levels. Then we need to begin realizing the true impact that our prejudices are having not only on ourselves but the world around us, no matter how small or insignificant we may think they are. What might seem a small prejudicial bias to someone might mean something much more devastating to the one that particular prejudice is being launched against!

Let not the perceived enlightenment of your soul come by embracing your prejudices that become a part of your everyday life. Rather take the approach of interaction with each and everyone that is part of not just your 'Tribe' or country or family or house of worship or political party, but rather everyone you encounter in any aspect of your daily life.

Love seems to be the ultimate form of human emotions and feelings but until it is tempered with Empathy for those that are different than one's self, it cannot be truly experienced by anyone! Your prejudices are building a wall between yourself and those around you preventing the exchange of pure feelings of human emotions on all levels, especially that of Love! Reduction of your prejudices greatly grows your ability to not only give, but to receive true Love on so many levels!

Vengeance and Revenge

Vengeance and revenge are emotions that are on such a low level of life I am surprised they made their way into our emotional or conceptual make up as humans. We must teach other people how to treat us; it is part of our development. We must show them that we are not aggressors that we all have territorial boundaries to our essence, our soul, that we respect theirs and they must respect ours, and that their territory ends where ours begins.

This does not discount retribution, for we must be accountable for our deeds and must make restitution to those that we have trespassed against or our conscience will weigh heavy against us and slow our journey in our spiritual growth.

If someone directs a form of being towards us that we are uneasy with, we must counteract it in the most logical way, but to a degree that allows a finite solution without the need for reprisals.

Vengeance and revenge take dearly from our treasure chest of stored emotions and deplete our energy. It is another way of harboring hate within our selves. It creates a continual, circular retribution style of dealing with facets of our experiences that are in reality of little or no value.

Inner Security

Inner security is the bundle of emotions that most of us do not recognize as one of our strongest values. We mistakenly believe it is a quality that is elusive, minute, forbidden to be a part of us most of the time. The sad thing is that our inner security is so abundant, so deep, and so meaningful. It is just the misconception, or misperception we have of this delightful emotion that prevents it from cradling our spirit on a continual basis.

We seem to feel that we are truly a lone entity within life and that we wander through our existence totally removed from our counterparts because we have bought into the identifying concept that we are a separate body, therefore we must be separated emotionally and spiritually. This premise is a fallacy for we are connected emotionally and spiritually with each and every other soul that exists or has ever existed.

We look so intensely at our bodily being that we remove our awareness from many facts and facets of our being. We are not alone on this earth or in this universe. We are one in identity, but are sharing a larger soul with all those around us. It is this inner 'direct sharing' of self that permeates our being and gives us hope and the feelings of belonging.

Each thought, each feeling, each tear is shared on a common ground with all. You alone do not shed a tear for it resonates to the ends of the universe and touches every other soul on its way. You may not be consciously aware of this fact here on earth, but that is just because you have tunneled your visionary concept of yourself as only a part of this existence. You have not allowed your mind to know what your inner soul does, that you are an inter-connected being with all life and its Creator.

With the whole of existence as a basic part of your being, inner security is a very powerful part of your essence. If you feel insecure, just relax and reach within your soul, turn away from your outward plight. Rest in the assurance that the totality of the makeup of mankind is there within your being to help you, to guide you, and to assist you in all your endeavors. With all that, the multitude of loving wealth that you have to tap into, your inner security is the most abundant emotion you possess.

Rainbow of Emotions

I think that all emotions have their place within our being. Just as the rainbow is a spectrum of many colors, each pleasing to one's eye, the culmination of all adds a true identity of a full life experience to any of us who allows themselves to bask in their totality.

Each emotion appears to be unique to one's self. We must remember that each emotion will touch us in a very special way. Perhaps no other soul has an exacting experience with the same degree of complexity or intensity as our perception of that feeling, that emotion, but countless others have felt it before you in some way or another.

You are not alone in your emotional world! Whatever has made you excited, elated, lonely, sad, fulfilled, tensed feelings or those of peace has touched a multitude of others. This does not discredit, negate, or lessen the burden of life's feelings and emotions upon you, but rather adds hope and credence to the fact that there is a way out of any emotional valley as so many others have found.

Nothing Lasts Forever

Nothing in life lasts forever, not good times, not bad times, nothing! When life seems dark and it appears that there is no tomorrow, no hope, no reprieve from your sadness, you must realize that even though you cannot see those emotional good times again at the moment, they will return. Once you have captured the essence of the value of the experience in your situation and you have learned from it you will grow in spirit. Once you question your stagnation of spirit and perceive it as a new direction rather than a stumbling block, you will rise above it. You will return centered with in your being and enlightened from your experiences rather than drained from them.

You must experience your emotions as they touch you. Life will never hand you an experience that you will not have the inner strength to face and or overcome! The worst thing that you can do for your physical, mental, and spiritual well being is to deny or suppress your emotions. Until they are addressed and worked out, they will haunt you in many ways. They can lay dormant within your being for many years and reveal themselves to you in negative fashions that will mask their true identity. The longer you deny or repress those emotions, the more devastating their effect will be on you and your life when they surface – and they will eventually surface.

Suppressing Your Emotions

I attended a funeral many years ago. It was for someone that I knew and loved very much. I entered the chapel where his family and friends were gathering to view the departed one. In an outer room sat an elderly woman, she was in her nineties. After viewing her great-grandson lying in his coffin, she was sitting on a sofa and was surrounded by some of her off spring of several generations.

Her great-grandson was laying in the next room in preparation to meet his maker. She was holding back a multitude of tears and it was obvious that the strain of the moment was more than she could emotionally endure. Her son told her to be brave, not to cry, and everything would be fine. He reiterated that she should not cry!

The room emptied as all but her and I went into the next room to view the departed once more. I turned to her; a stranger I had not met before, and in my heart I knew just what she needed.

My mind raced back to the death of one of my older brother's and how a member of my family told me to 'be brave and not to cry at his funeral.' I was told that I must be strong for my parents and those around me. I was only around twelve years old at the time and this was the first death in our rather large family of sixteen children I had ever experienced. It was also the first and only funeral I had ever attended.

I was strong. I did hold back my tears. I held them back for years and years and even decades. They haunted me as I suppressed them. They returned to me in dreams. They finally took such a hold on me that I was unable to sleep. I could not understand what was happening to me. I had not correlated my draining of strength of soul and being to the fact that I had not dealt with my feelings and emotions of my brother's death. It was years after losing my brother that I finally was able to face the feelings, the emotions that I needed to and broke down and cried.

Here in front of me was a great-grand mother in her nineties. Here was a soul that was having the same mistaken perception of strength or 'be brave and do not cry' pushed upon her to keep her from dealing with the emotions that were boiling up inside her.

I sat down beside this stranger. I put my arm around her and held her hand and looked into her eyes. I was not only looking into her eyes, but her very soul and whispered to her that it was okay to cry.

I knew that was what she needed. I knew that was what her soul craved at that moment. I did not want to see her carry her tears to her grave and never be at peace because she was forced into the fallacy that being strong meant stifling your soul and holding back your feelings and emotions that needed to be faced, accepted, and put to rest!

As she looked back at me her eyes were sort of clouded and she looked a bit confused. I could see that she was holding her emotions back with all her strength. Once she saw my tears, once she knew that it was alright and safe to show me her emotions, she said to me that she loved her great-grandson so much and she wanted to cry for him as well. I held her tight as the tears streamed down her face and she leaned on my shoulder clutching me as though I were a safe port in her great emotional storm.

When she started to compose herself, I knew she was not ready yet. I told her again that it was all right to cry and that her great grandson would want her to. Again she wept as I held her tight.

Moments later she did compose herself just as the family was starting to return to the room we were in. She looked at me again and told me that she felt better about her great grandson and that she knew in her heart that he would be all right and that he is resting in peace in heaven. She then thanked me for allowing her to cry.

Can you imagine that? We are so closed with our emotions that she had been first told to suppress her emotions and feelings, and now she was **'thankful'** that someone had the insight and sensitivity to encourage her to accept her emotions, her hurts, her loss, and allowed her to begin the healing process of accepting what happened to great-grandson and let her cry!

Why are we so afraid of expressing our emotions that we need permission from a stranger in order to cry? To allow the hurt of one's loss of a loved one to go repressed will only add to their burden of loss. It is only through the true tears you express that will cleanse one's soul and give you peace in times such as these.

During the short time we shared that emotional experience, a soul-to-soul bond developed between that elderly lady and myself. Here was another soul that new the meaning of facing and dealing with their emotions even though it was not the accepted norm of the social premise at hand.

You must be able to control and handle certain negative emotions in order to keep life in balance. Hatred, revenge, jealousy, and emotions of this nature must also be dealt with, but not experienced as an ultimate manifestation, but understood and diffused.

Emotions from the loss of a loved one, perceived loneliness, and insecurity due to oppression must be experienced. There are basic paths the psychic follows in order to heal one's emotions.

First there is the denial - it never happened!

Then there is anger - how could it happen, and why to me?

Then isolation and self-denial be it physical, emotional, or spiritual.

This is followed by the ultimate grieving process of crying, and finally the soul perceives new insights, sets new goals for itself, and starts healing.

If you truly deal effectively with your emotions, your healing process will cause a strengthening factor within your soul and you will be a better person for it. Other people can nurture you through these tough times, but you must experience the emotions yourself.

Sharing Your Emotions And Feelings

You need a confidant in life, one that you can reveal your inner feelings to, knowing that they are considered sacred to that person and are not to be revealed to anyone else, ever! The sharing of your emotions is the best way to understand and deal with them. In order to tell someone else of your feelings, you have to formalize them in your mind and you have to put conceptual value to them. Once you do this, once you speak them out loud or write them down, you will see them in a different perspective.

If you share your emotions and feelings with another caring soul, their intensity is diffused. If you have no one to confide in, write your feelings and emotions down, get them out so you can start dealing with them. You will never find a solution to a problem until you clearly know what the problem is. Many times it is the unclear perception of a problem that makes it persist.

Finding A Confidant

The best way to find a confidant in life is to be one, just as the best way to find a friend is to be one. You must be able to listen to another's problems with sincerity. You must be attentive to them, but not heed their healing process by interjecting your answers to their problems.

No one can resolve another's emotional turmoil. They can assist in guidance, reassurance, and a display of concern and caring, but they cannot resolve the inner conflict within you. You must learn to allow others to freely express their own feelings and emotions just as I did with that great grandmother. I told her it was all right for her to show her emotions to me and that I was not judging her. I was simply there to help her 'be with' her inner feelings.

The only intervention I displayed was encouraging her to keep the emotions coming as long as she needed to cry. We have mechanisms within ourselves that makes us want to turn off our emotions. When someone has the courage to finally face their emotions, they should be encouraged to experience them totally.

Our mind is so unique and clever that it will only allow us to face the amount of emotions that we can handle within a given time frame. It will only allow that if it feels we are in an emotionally safe environment. You should never push yourself or anyone else beyond that point that they are ready to face. This leaves a fine line, you must be sensitive enough to determine if their emotions have stopped because a person displaying them has pulled back unnecessarily because of social negative perceptions of their display or they have reached the saturation point and have no more strength to face or deal with their emotional situation at that moment in time.

Your emotions will be dealt with whether you want them to or not. If you deny them, they will haunt you in some fashion. They will continue to affect you until you face them and dissipate their effect on you by letting them evolve away from your being into their own dimension.

The emotions you suppress will make themselves known a little at a time. You will be able to handle them, even if it means facing the loss of a loved one. Only when you face your emotions will they be resolved. If you deny them, they will appear to leave you, but they will only cycle deep within your mind and soul and there they will grow and become hardened or confused while waiting for your acceptance.

Don't make the mistake of denial that I did of my deeper emotions. Life will fool you. You will feel that you have taken charge by denial, that you are able to suppress your being, that you are a man or woman enough to not allow yourself to be 'weak' and cry or do whatever it is necessary to positively deal with your emotions.

I feel it is the 'weak' that do not cry or face their feelings in some way when life has dealt them a tremendous blow. Only by releasing our emotions does their clouding effect over our being, our soul, dissipate allowing our true inner strength to manifest.

You must remember that life is a beautiful experience and unlike most of us have been led to believe, we are here to experience it in a happy and fulfilling state. The true natural state of being for us is that of gentle repose, contentment, and happiness within our being. We are told endlessly how we must suffer life to grow from it. True, we do grow from life's pains, but we should not expect to create a life of pain so we can feel our growth.

Life will deal each and every one of us their share of its pains for growth. You do not have to seek them out. You must set your emotional goals towards a positive and happy plain. You should be happy most of the time. If you are not, then it is time to reflect within yourself and re-orient your life in ways that happiness becomes a normal state for you.

Resiliency With Your Emotions

You must develop a sense of resiliency with your emotions. You must face your feelings, deal with them effectively, but don't hold on to them too long, for they are there to teach you how to breathe life in, not to stop it. We must realize that our inner goal is to be happy and we must return to that state as quickly as we can after our experience with our emotions has worked itself out. We must not linger on the path of recovery. Life is momentary and we must capture its essence to its fullness, not stopping our soul too long while journeying down its path.

Many of us would rather be martyrs than be happy. We burden ourselves for others in the mistaken belief that through all that suffering we are a better person and will receive a better place in the next life. Your life is meant to be lived **now** by you. You must do what you can to help others in their plight in life, but you must also find happiness in yours and yourself. You must not let anyone else suppress or repress your enlightened experience here with in your own life's experience!

You must not let other's negatives become your own. You must not accept any negatives from within or without your own being. Do not accept the negative perceptions, comments, gestures, or antics of others. You are unique within yourself, special, and should let no one judge you.

We are so conditioned to negatives that we subconsciously tell ourselves **'no'** thousands of times over. We must restructure that voice with in us, the one that always looks for the dark side of any situation and turn it towards more positive perceptions of our being and our life.

Our subconscious mind is a very powerful thing. It is very goal oriented and will strive for and attain any goal we come to believe in. This is true of our emotional makeup also. If we wish to be happy with our life, our emotions, feel good most of the time, then we must reach for those perceptions and stop kidding ourselves that some outward force is going to hand it to us.

It is a hard realization to face, that of being responsible for one's own emotional experience. But once you do, once you take control and perceive that you are indeed in control, you will feel the grandeur of self as you have never felt it before. You will also find inner security more abundant as you are no longer relying on external forces for people to make you 'feel' life, as **you** want it.

Experience All Of Your Emotions

Be thankful that you have the ability and the insight to experience all of your emotions. It is better to be able to laugh and cry than to be hardened to this beautiful experience we call life. Those who harden themselves emotionally by entering into protective shells will never experience the enlightenment of life that you will. Don't be afraid of your emotions. Don't suppress them or wish they would go away. They are an integral part of you. They are one of the cherished things that you will be allowed to take with you when your perception of life ends on this plain and you travel your spirit onto whatever levels of life or existence you perceive is the next step in your development.

The New Emotion

We must reach into our very essence for a moment now and re-kindle a feeling that has been bred into submission by centuries of locking our focal point onto the reality we perceived as the totality of our make up. There is another emotion beyond love, hate, sharing, greed, empathy, or any emotional value that you might hold dear to your heart. We have tunneled not only our intellectual visions into a distorted consortium of real perception, but that of our emotional values as well.

Once you realize the true identity of yourself is a part of a larger entity that is unlike anything you can imagine you will begin to understand. It is as though you are a single cell of a larger being. Your identity remains in accord as any cell, developing a purpose and reason, and adding to your own growths and strengths, but also enhancing the larger entity. Once you realize that we are a part of a grand being, that this life is but one vision that we share in our unending life pattern, you will understand the new emotion I am about to speak of.

You must imagine yourself not in the factors that you have come to believe. You must relinquish all your normal factors of accountability of existence and reality and reach out with your thoughts to the possibility and probability that the real factions of life are not based with in your present existence. You must dare to challenge your very make up, your very intellectual, spiritual, ethical, and physical being, realizing only by re-focusing your thoughts can you achieve the understanding of what is in fact your soul, and therefore be able to understand and enhance your development and individuality as a whole and complete being.

Your true existence is not here in this reality. You are a part of another existence that is a direct part of the whole universal concept of totality. Your life here can be likened to a picture in a gallery. You have focused your attention here to study, learn from, and admire, but you are only focusing your attention creating this illusion. As with any great painting you might see things within it that others would not. You may wish to study it more than others, but you are limited to your stay for the sake of your soul's growth pattern. When your counter parts, be they family or friend die, it is because they have removed their focus from this illusion, this piece of art and have moved onto another.

You are in communication with each and every cell in the whole of the universe. Each individually viewing out into various realities at various stages of their wanting. You share a common bond within the whole structure, a communicable, sharing, and loving bond. It is this other awareness, this 'direct sharing' bond that is truly the other emotion that I am speaking of.

We bind ourselves by certain agreed laws from the whole of our experience of life. These laws are agreed upon, but are not permanent. Each soul in this plain, each sensitive being within our realm that can reach out, turn their focus away from this existence, can indeed see through the laws of reality, physics, and the binding norms that we have stifled our ways and our wills with.

By removing our focus from this dimension and by reaching our soul in another direction, we can in fact have 'direct sharing' of our essence with any and all the other cells of the universe. This is a factor that takes place continually, but by having our direct focus so tightly bound to this existence, we are unaware except on occasion, of this 'direct sharing' of essence, intelligence, creativity, and emotions.

Validation of this concept is simple. This explains why throughout our history minds in different regions have conceived exacting inventions, similar values in religion, writings, and various other factors that appear as a commonality even though no direct interplay of knowledge was conceivable.

This concept will add a great deal of comfort to anyone that truly comprehends and accepts it. If you study this premise without malice or wittingly trying to disprove it, you will feel the revelations that I am speaking of. You will relish in a new dawn within your soul and intellect. You will understand your soul, your life, and your inner being much better.

You will also understand why your loved ones pass from your life, comforted by the realization that you are nestled closely together as you have always been. You are bound together by your emotions, your feelings, your love, in a true reality that is an all encompassing, never ending realm of spiritual growth.

You will not hold too tightly to the memories of loss when you realize they are only perceptual to you at this moment. As you fade from this existence, your fellow treasures will return to your awareness and the only factor you lost was the moment that you kept your attention on the short realization of existence here, rather than in your overall view of life.

Your love and your loved ones pass not from your existence, but rather from your momentary conceptual awareness. This current factor is only a part of reality because you have chosen not to question its validity, and reached within your soul and allowed exchange with those that have turned their perceptions towards a new direction.

Once you can conceive, comprehend, and utilize the concept of 'direct sharing' you and our culture will be able to make great strides within our social structure on intellectual as well as spiritual values.

If all the emotions, all the intelligence, all the forethought, all the creativity of every soul that ever existed or will ever exist was directed towards the solution, the creation, the perception of any problem or factor within our current realm, there would be nothing that could not be enhanced, overcome, or solved.

It is this premise that I am making you aware of as a real concept that is in place within our universal structure. We but need to only realize the validity of it and put some real effort into its utilization.

Anything that we can perceive, anything that we can believe, anything that we can surmise can in some ways become a reality if we collectively conceive it as a new direction for our culture. We must realize that we solemnly and collectively create our lives and our existence.

We are not at the whims of the stars or the resonating factors of numerical vibrations, but rather we create the harmonious balance that is in fact the reality of our conceived and perceived universe.

We individually are an active participant in our existence and can and do have control and effect upon our being. We have this effect both positively and negatively. It is the negative factors that truly stifle our intellectual and spiritual growth. Negative emotions seem to have a much more resounding effect on us than our positive emotions because of our negative mind set that was created as a learning guide for our development from adolescence to maturity. The **no** responses that were given us as feedback to chart our growth into a positive pattern were considered a positive way for our intellectual and spiritual growth.

This is a rather absurd concept necessary in part, but the negative responses far overshadow the positive. This means we are more set into a faction of intellect that adheres to the premise that negatives are the primary set of guidelines to follow. This creates a global mindset that is hard to counter until there comes an awareness that causes a situation allowing redirection of our awareness to a more positive direction.

There is nothing that we collectively conceive that will not come to pass if we but change our hearts' reach from what we fear to what we cherish. The 'new tomorrows' will only be enhanced over today by our awareness of this 'direct sharing' of self, knowledge, and soul. The combining effect will allow us the sensitivity to enhance ourselves, have empathy to help others in their plight, and give us the responsibility to become a global being reaching forward for growth of being, enhanced intellectual perceptions, rather than our personal greed's be they physical or emotional.

AND UNDERSTANDING ONE'S SELF

You cannot experience your emotions, you cannot travel down life's path without coming into an understanding, and a realization of one's self, whatever that concept may be. We are a culmination of every part of 'us' that has ever been, is, or forever will be. Life touches us as we go through it, and all that touching remains a subtle or deep part of our being.

The reason life seems hard to understand at times is the fact that we spend so little time reflecting within our soul, listening to our hearts, our inner thoughts, wishes, and wants. We cloud our make up with so many superficial things that the items we cherish are sought more from competition rather than endearment.

The little boy or little girl that you once were is still a part of the wonderful being you are this very day. Some of the perceptions you have of this life are still reflected in your life through the eyes of those little children that are still playing within your being. It is grand that every part of you truly does remain in tact, for if not, life would harden us and we would evolve into meaningless characters without the ability to love.

You must give time in life for your inner reflections. You must learn to relax your being each day, giving yourself time to calmly take store of your aspirations, your hopes, your goals, your wants, your fears, your past, present and future. It's these little moments of relaxing your mind and reaching within yourself that will add much strength and insight to your being. You can easily find time in your day for some or all of your chores. Just as easily, you can find a few moments for yourself in solitude so you can relax, reflect, and regroup yourself.

Understanding one's self comes from reflecting upon life. You must take the time and enjoy the memories you have of your life.

They are precious assets that can never be replaced. Remember the good times; reflect on your moments of strength, love, replaying them within your mind like a wonderful motion picture of your being. Step into this picture in your mind and relive those experiences. Then turn your thoughts forward and envision your future in the positive and loving manner you want it to become. These slices of reflection within your day will add new strengths, new insights, and new vitality to you physically, mentally, and spiritually.

Remember the special being that you are, the wonderful person that is you and only you, the unique soul that you are. See that life is meant to be a glorious experience and that you are to learn from it, learn to love it, and be an active participant in it and your dreams.

Take this time to give yourself the affirmations that you lack from those around you. You have the right to recognize the special qualities that are in your make up. During this time, dwell only on the positive things of your being as we are bombarded with negative emotions and feelings from so many sources constantly.

Cherish what is you! Reflect a more positive view if you wish, but only because it is with this change of view, this belief in a better self that you will attain that change.

You must change your dreams to fit today. You must take active charge of your inner feelings and emotions. **You must not follow another's dreams for your own are so beautiful!**

Things seem to burden us, but it is our concept of reality and not so much reality itself that causes our concerns. Everything we experience, every aspect of our lives whether we view them as good or bad are meant in some way for our development as an individual or our interactions, be they acceptance, rejection, or what with others. We must not dwell on the suffering we conceive or the fear we foresee. We need to view life as a whole being and realize that any problems we face are for a short period only and that we are faced with no problem that life has not given us the answer to and the means to overcome at some point.

When Love Ceases To Be Love

Love ceases to be love when it becomes dependency. We need to grasp the now moments of our lives and be kind and gentle to ourselves. The past must remain unchanged, as it is forever gone. We can cherish the good thoughts, but must not let the past sadden our grasp of life this moment, nor should the future keep us from living fully in the now. Most of what we fear will never happen but in our thoughts, so it is necessary to look to the future only with kind and subtle expectations and enjoy the beauty you are and have now.

Build Ourselves Up

We must learn to build ourselves up, to be kind to ourselves, compliment and encourage ourselves. What we do easily for others, we find difficult to do for ourselves. We are worthy of this same love and kindness.

We must learn to take life easy and to view things completely before making rush decisions. Life gives us time if we make ourselves aware of this fact. Give yourself and your life the time it needs.

The Least Bit of Love

The least bit of love resonates throughout the universe as a pebble dropped in a calm pool ripples its effects to the outermost parts of its being. There is a common bond or force running true to form throughout love, music, touch, warmth, and peace. It is a common vibration that parallels the natural pulse of the universe. Harmonizing one's self with any or all of those forces enables you to tap into the secrets of the universe.

Be Yourself

If you have a tormented mind, be yourself! Don't let the social standards of how you should live destroy the love and soul within you.   Remember to be yourself is to be at peace. If you find peace but a moment at a time, cherish it, for that moment is the joy, the echo of your destiny for all time.

If today seems a burden, remember that due to the complex cycle of life and growth, a cell must die now and then, but in truth it only comes to pass because a new growth in your manifestation is being revealed. Sorrow is just a gentle and temporary void between your two universes of good.

Finding Peace

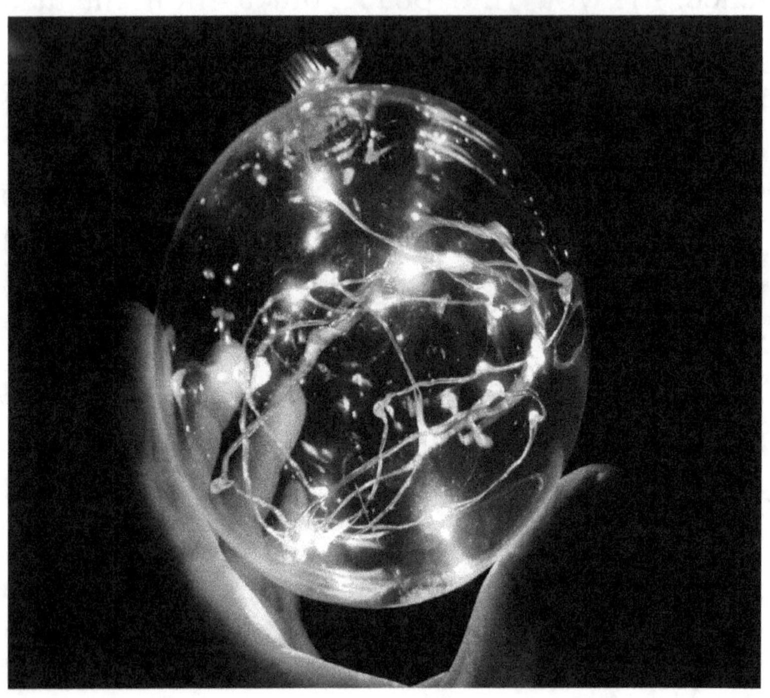

I found peace when I realized I am not just for today, so I do not need to prove my whole world or worth in just twenty-four hours. That is how life is to be lived, in the now. You must plan for your future, you must dream your dreams and reach for them, but you are only asked to live this day, this moment, this life one second at a time. Cherish that fact, for it will protect you from many of your fears. The future, no matter how bleak you may perceive it cannot enter your 'now' and disturb you unless you let it.

Be Happy

You must learn to be happy this moment without a condition to make it so. Most people live life on the differed payment plan. They will be happy at some time in the future because of an event, or acquiring something for their being, be it physical, emotional, or spiritual. Each day must be enjoyed as a separate entity.

You cannot live in the tomorrow. Your journey through life is your real reason for living. The striving for your goals and the dreams you create and partake in are the source that gives you and your life meaning and reward.

Life and dreams are in fact one. You live in one and are the other. Take the time to make them what you wish them to be. Learn of yourself by reflecting upon your life and understanding one's self. Change your life and your destiny to fit the way you want life to touch you.

Happiness

Within your chest rises now and then a warm and welcomed feeling of repose and serenity. It begins with a mind at peace and grows into excitement for life. It continues to flow through your veins, warming your soul to far beyond the temperature of just being alive. This trait has been labeled 'happiness.'

This force can be brought forth at anytime you want to really depart from your past or present woes. Be alive, breathe in the goodness of the ages and expel your cares. Let the world just sort of float away. Let its' cares gently settle into the past. Relax and count your good times in your mind.

Thank the Universe for your very being. Let go of your troubles or torments and be the one you have always wanted to be even if just for a moment. Let the smile from deep within your contented soul gently appear across your face letting yourself and others know of your state of happiness.

Animals Have Emotions and Feelings Too!

As long as we are on the subject of Emotions and Feelings I firmly believe, as many of you I am sure do as well, that the human species does not have exclusivity when it comes to emotions and feelings and expressing them. The animal kingdom does so as well and on many levels.

They of course do not have the ability to express their various feelings and emotional bonds, as we humans do, being void of interspecies speech. They can and do express their feelings and emotions not only to and from humans, but deep within their own species and with other species as well.

Animals of course have had to adapt to their human counterparts in different ways of communicating their rainbow array of feelings that any dog, cat, or other domesticated pet owner can attest too. That lick on your hand or face, that attentive look at you, that snuggle against you as you lay on the couch or in bed, that frolic and frisky way they greet you and the many other attributes they display show their emotional attachment to you. They can also express feelings of insecurity and fear when confronted with a negative scolding or the worst of all, any form of physical or emotional abuse by humans.

Animals are a comfort to us in so many ways. They are all forgiving, attentive, loving, and comforting when we need those things in our lives most. During this time of physical separation of social distancing, we can take comfort, solace, peace, and harmony in a turned upside down world by gently petting or letting them nap on our laps as we try to deal with all of life's current problems.

For those of you that might not fully accept that animals can relate in their emotions and feelings across species lines, and to further point out that animals can and do have and express a wide variety of emotions and feelings, I would like to share a true story that will without a doubt solidify my belief that animals of all kinds share emotional values and feelings likened to ours.

The following story happened when I was a young lad growing up on a farm in northern Idaho in the early 1960's. Years later I put this story in a book about our family for my Parent's Sixtieth Wedding Anniversary. It was written to keep many of the memories of them and their sixteen children that had happened throughout their years of raising such a large family from being forgotten.

I feel it spells out the interconnection of emotions and feelings between we as humans and our beloved pets as well as those in nature. Hopefully it will give you insight into the bond you share with your pets and other animals and make you realize the importance of that bond of love that animals both domestic and in the wild can help us through these turbulent emotional times.

Relax and let your mind wander from your stress and current problems for a while. Journey back with me to a more relaxed and pleasant time, one that will give you hope and strength now by learning from the bond of love between two animals that transcended their trials and tribulations long ago.

PAWNEE
A DEER WITH A HEART
By Jerry W. Miller
1960

It all began one day during haying season back on the farm where I grew up as a boy in northern Idaho near a town named Bonners

Ferry. We had to harvest our hay loose because we could not afford a hay bailer. My brother Joe and I were getting the last couple of loads of hay in before a summer storm was about to hit. The rest of the family had been out helping us the day before and earlier that morning, but they had to go into town for food and supplies. They figured Joe and I could handle what was left in the fields.

We used a small John Deer tractor and a trailer that my father had made from the axel of an old car and some boards off one of our old sheds, to haul the hay with. It was hard for me to drive the tractor because I was so small I could barely reach the pedals with my feet. On the farm you learned how to run equipment at an early age, when the crops were ready to be put in or harvested. All hands were needed to do the job quickly.

We had an old dump rake that would pile the loose hay up into large stacks. Then we merely had to drive the tractor and trailer down the rows of haystacks and pitch the loose alfalfa or clover onto the trailer. Joe was older and slightly stronger than I was, so I left most of the hay pitching to him.

We gathered up a full load of hay and was about to head back to the barn because the sky had filled with large black clouds and it was about to rain at any moment. Joe spotted something in the woods beside the hay field.

"Look at that!" He exclaimed, as he pointed into the thick underbrush. "It's a fawn, I wonder where its mother the doe is?"

"Wow!" Was all I could say. I loved to see deer in nature. They are so sleek and graceful. When they run they are so poetic in their every move. "That's funny, the deer doesn't seem to be afraid of us!" I commented.

The fawn came sprinting out of the woods and walked right up to our wagonload of hay. It then started chewing some of the freshly dried clover from it.

"I don't believe it!" Joe remarked as he laid his pitchfork down and stared in awe.

At that, I slowly walked up to the little deer, stretched out my hand and gently and softly ran my fingers down the back of the fawn's neck. The deer did not flinch, instead it continued right on about its business of consuming our hay. I patted it on the side like I sometimes did our pet dog and rubbed his neck.

By this time Joe had approached and was also petting the deer as well. The deer did not mind all this attention from the two of us; in fact it enjoyed the caressing. It looked as though it had lacked food for sometime because his little ribs were showing.

"Look at this!" my brother yelled. He had ventured farther into the thicket of woods from where the fawn had made its appearance.

I ran over to see what he had found, and sure enough there on its' side was a large deer. "Is it the fawn's mother?" I asked. "Poor thing, what happened to it?"

Joe responded, "Yes, it is the fawn's mother! Look here, there is blood on the ground."

Sure enough, there was a pool of dried blood on the ground near the deer's neck. Joe grabbed the deer by the head and twisted it slightly over, exposing a wound from a hunter's bullet. The sight made me sick. I hated to see anything in nature killed, especially something so beautiful as a wild deer.

"It would not be so bad if they would have tracked down the deer and kept if for meat!" Joe went on. "But to kill a deer like that and just let it die and rot out here is such a waste. Not only that, maybe the hunter could not track it down after he shot it, but there was no excuse for the deer being killed anyway, because it was not even deer hunting season. That means that whoever shot this deer did it illegally."

Seasons are put on wild animals to protect their life cycle. For instance, a deer hunting season is usually begun in the late fall because the mother deer usually give birth to their fawns in the early spring. During the summer, the fawns grow enough so they can take care of themselves in the event their mother might be killed during hunting season. In this case, the mother had just given birth not more than a couple of months ago before she had been killed.

The fawn, still bearing spots, was unable to fend for itself. Sure, he could feed and water himself minus his mother's milk, but he was left at the mercy of any wild animals. A wandering wolf, cougar, or even a farmer's dog threatened its very existence with out the protection of its mother watching over it.

"What are we going to do?" I asked. "Can we just leave the fawn here to die, or should we tie it up and take it with us?"

Joe's reply was, "If we tie up a wild creature like that and take it home it would be against the law. All we can do is hope that the fawn makes out okay by itself."

Just then the clouds began letting go of their heavy load and it began to rain hard. We decided we had better go. If you allow loose hay to get wet before you put it in the barn, during the winter months the hay will "sweat," or get real hot all by itself and can start a fire through the process of spontaneous combustion. Many a farmer has lost his barn to fire because of this.

My brother jumped onto the tractor and I climbed up on the load of loose hay, and off we started. I looked down at the deer chewing on a bunch of hay that had fallen from the load when we started off. I felt pity for that poor little creature. What had it done wrong to deserve being left in the world all alone to fend for itself? How could anyone get pleasure from shooting its poor mother and then just leave her there to die?

I waved good by to the fawn, and yelled, "Good luck, and I hope nature takes care of you."

The deer rose up its head with its ears standing on end and looked at me as though it had understood every word I had said. Then realizing that we were leaving, it quickly finished up the bit of hay on the ground in front of it and started to follow our overflowing with fresh hay trailer.

I called to my brother, "Don't go too fast, we have a straggler following us."

It was neat, the fawn followed us all the way home, chewing off the hay draping from the side of our trailer the entire trip. As we pulled up next to the barn, the folks and the rest of the family had just returned from town.

They came running to the barn when they saw the fawn still eating from the load of hay. My brothers and sisters flocked around him like a group of children would an ice cream wagon. The deer showed no fear, not even when our pet dog Spike came up and sniffed him. We decided then and there that we were going to keep him for a family pet permanently, or so we thought.

Spike

The amazing thing about the entire thing was how much our pet border collie Spike took to that little fawn. They ate together, they slept beside each other, and they played together just like two little puppies would. The dog would lick the deer on the nose, and the deer would smooth down the long hair on the dogs neck with his tongue. They played and frolicked in the near by fields and had so much fun together.

I thought it was funny when they chased each other back and forth around the farm just like two little children playing. The dog would chase the deer up the wooded hillside by the house and five minutes later, the deer would be chasing Spike back down the hill.

It was all in fun, but represented a serious problem because in farm country like north Idaho, it was one of the greatest crimes a dog could commit, that of chasing deer. Once a dog starts to chase deer, it might very well likely round up a pack of other dogs and as a gang they will go out and chase a deer until it drops from exhaustion, then kill it.

We were afraid that someone might spot Spike chasing our pet deer and think he was chasing him to kill it, rather than just playing with him. The unwritten code in our part of the country back then was to shoot-on-sight any dog seen chasing a deer. If by some chance someone spotted them and did not know of their relationship, it could have been fatal for Spike.

A bond of friendship grew between those two animals that was stronger than any bond of love or friendship that I have ever seen. They became so much a part of one another that they were inseparable. They really showed how nature had mastered the art of love between its children even between different species.

It took our family almost two and a half weeks to decide on a name for our new pet deer. Remember at that time there was at least a dozen plus children and a couple adults all vying for the best name for the creature. Some of our older brothers and sisters had already left home to start lives of their own. It seemed that no matter what the choice might be, one or more of us did not like it for some reason. We finally settled on "Pawnee" as the most unique name for him.

One hot and sulky summer evening the whole family was in the living room watching television. Since it was so hot, we left all the windows and doors wide open. We had just finished supper, but the dishes were still on the table. Mom and one of my sisters had decided to wait until it cooled off a little in the kitchen before they attempted to clear them up off the table.

We were half way through a second rate movie when Mom heard something in the kitchen. It sounded like a plate had fallen from the table, but she was not alarmed enough to bother investigating the noise. Then all of a sudden a loud crash echoed from the kitchen, startling all of us. We hurried into the kitchen to find our table knocked on its side and everything left from the evening meal smashed to the floor. There in the midst of it all stood Pawnee licking the butter plate. He had evidently knocked one of the wooden legs out from under the table and it had turned over on its side.

I looked at Mom and Dad expecting them to be furious, but they were both ready to burst out laughing. Here was a deer in our kitchen with spaghetti strands hanging down from his neck and head, his right front leg covered with tomato sauce, and standing with all four hoofs in a pool of milk. His eyes were dilated as though he was in shock. Mom shooed him out of the kitchen and we all cleaned up the mess.

"If that deer keeps up his mischievous ways, he will have to go!" Mom mumbled as she swept up the last shattered pieces of her broken dishes.

"You don't mean that Mom? Do you?" I remarked. "We couldn't ever let Pawnee go!"

"I was just kidding." She replied. "But you must remember that we will not be able to keep him as a pet forever. You do know don't you that deer kept in captivity or used for pets can turn wild after a couple of years and become dangerous to be around? They have very sharp hoofs and could easily kill a person."

I replied. "Pawnee would never do anything like that!"

"Maybe not, Jerry, but remember that Pawnee won't be around forever."

That remark bothered me. The fact that someday we might lose our precious pet was heartbreaking to a young boy. We played with Pawnee like children would play with any other pet. We would go on hikes and picnics in the woods near our farm and it was common thought that Pawnee and Spike would always go along with us. Every morning Pawnee and Spike would meet me at the door. They would welcome in the new day as I opened it and handed them both some food. Pawnee would eat any scraps from the table, which made it convenient because he and Spike shared the same eating bowl.

One morning all I feared of possibly losing Pawnee came to light when I opened up the door with their food and they were not there to greet me. I ran out into the front yard calling their names, but they were absolutely nowhere to be found.

The rest of our household joined in the search, but to no avail. This was the first time that they had left on their own like that. We could not help but wonder if something serious had happened to them.

We reluctantly walked up to the highway to catch the school bus. Since this was our last day of school and we were just going in for a couple of hours to pick up our report cards. Mom decided we had better not miss our last day of school for the year.

By the time we returned home, Pawnee and Spike had not shown up yet. I could not help but think that the deer had returned to the wilderness to find a life with nature. Maybe the call of nature had indeed bitten into his soul and returned him to her bounds. But then, why was our dog Spike gone as well? He would have no intentions of leaving the shelter of his home for a life in the wilderness that he knew nothing about.

All our worries of what might have happened were shattered by the horror of what really had happened when Mom received a phone call from the local Game Warden.

"Mrs. Miller you had better get over to the Moyie Springs gravel pits real quick! Your pet deer and dog are over there and there is a pack of dogs chasing them." He told my mother. "I received a call from Mrs. Turner of

Moyie Springs. She was passing by the gravel pits on her way back home from Bonners Ferry and saw them. She was too frightened to get out of the car and help them out, so she called me. I figured you are closer and could reach them faster than I can."

All my Mom could say was a quick, "Thank you. I'll get over there right away!" She slammed down the receiver and hollered at us children to get into the car.

Off we went. We all piled into an old beetle back style 1949 Chevy that was on its last legs. Mom who was sometimes referred to as the terror of the highway by us, wound that old car up so fast that I thought the tires were going to burn off. We went over seven miles of the most abused and ill kept highways in north Idaho, and arrived at the gravel pits in much less than ten minutes.

The gravel pits consisted of high piles of gravel used to resurface roads and sand to spread on the snow in the winter to make the icy roads passable. Some of the piles were as high as a two or three story house.

Pawnee and Spike were at the top of the highest pile of gravel. It was sort of leveled off on top so they had a place to stand. Spike had Pawnee at the center of the top and was forming a protective circle around him. He was fighting off a pack of six dogs. He was a rather small dog, but he was King of the whole animal world that day for that little pup was endangering his life for that little deer.

One of the dogs broke through the line and bit deeply into Pawnee's side. Spike snarled at the dog and lunged his teeth deep into the wolf like dog's neck. With the power of a bear trap, Spike snapped the tormentor's neck. As the dog fell, it pulled away a large chunk of hair and flesh from Pawnee's side.

The sight of the blood excited the other dogs enough that they were ready to break the line and rush in for the kill. Just then Mom laid her hand on the car's horn. We children jumped out of the car, not fearing the immediate danger, but instead were running towards Pawnee and Spike screaming and throwing anything we could get a hold of at those attacking dogs.

All the commotion and rock and stick throwing scared off the pack of dogs. We headed up the pile of gravel. There at the top was Pawnee lying on his side with blood gushing from his stomach area. Spike lay whimpering by his side and was licking Pawnee's forehead. As I approached the scene I was struck in awe as never before had I imagined that such devotion could be engendered within the hearts of two supposedly non-emotional animals as those two.

Here our pet dog Spike, a common border collie, had fought and killed of his own kind to save his friend's life. Here he lay bleeding from the many cuts incurred from the battle. Instead of thinking of his own wounds, he was whimpering over and nursing his best friend, an animal not even a member of his own species.

It was this sight that made me realize for the first time that deep love truly existed throughout the realm of nature as well as mankind. It also showed that perhaps mankind was not the ultimate being when it came to emotions, feelings and expressions of love.

Mom finally reached the top of the gravel mound. She is the type that is filled with deep emotions and sympathy, but is gifted with the ability to subdue her emotions during an emergency. Rather than weeping at the sight like all us children were doing, she immediately started to help out the situation. She tore a long patch from the bottom of her slip and folded it gently against Pawnee's side in hopes to stop the bleeding. She then instructed Joe and I to give her our belts, which she linked together as a means to hold the bandage securely around Pawnee's side.

She instructed us to carefully lift Pawnee up and slowly carry him down from the mound. Spike followed us closely. Several times I felt that I was going to burst out into tears for Spike would let out some of the most heart broken whimpers that I have ever heard coming from an animal before.

We arrived at the car and gently placed Pawnee in the back seat. We let Spike lay down on the floor next to him. The rest of us crowded into the front seat and off we sped for home.

Mom said, "I just wish we could afford to take them both to the vet, but we just can't afford it. We will have to bandage them up the best we can and leave the rest in the Lord's hands."

I thought to myself, "Why do things like this have to happen to us? Why were we not able to afford a vet?   Why in this world of abundance should our pets die just because we could not afford to have then properly cared for?"

I of course, being so young, could not comprehend the monetary toll that my mother and father were enduring while raising sixteen children. Dad worked in heavy construction driving a large dozer, but there were seasonal times when jobs were scarce, so every dollar was precious to maintain our farm and place food on the table for so many of us. It was only during an extreme emergency that we could afford to be taken to a doctor when I was young, let alone having the money to pay for a veterinarian.

We arrived home and carried Pawnee into the house. Spike was never allowed in the house for it was family policy not to let any pet in our home. When he followed us in this time, not a word was said by any of us, including Mom.

Mom gave instructions to my sister to boil some water and bring her medicine and gauze from the medicine chest. She made a solution of warm water and boric acid (a mild medicine used to sterilize cuts and scrapes) and gently sponged out the wounds on Pawnee and Spike. She then put a dry bandage of gauze on the wound and surrounded Pawnee's whole body with another strip of gauze to hold the bandage securely in place.

Pawnee never flinched once through this whole painful ordeal. He knew that Mom was trying her best to help him. Spike stayed by his side through it all, licking Pawnee's face once in a while as if to say, "You will be alright now, you will be alright."

"Is he going to live Mom?" I asked. "Is he going to make it?"

"I can't say. He has lost a lot of blood!" Was her reply. "He is in for a rough time. I expect him to get much weaker in the next few days. If he can just hold on for awhile and give his body a chance to replace some of the lost blood, he will be alright."

The next three days were torture for the entire family, including the family dog. Pawnee just lay their hardly moving even an eyelash. He refused to eat or do anything. There by his side was Spike, just as motionless. We tried to feed Pawnee, but he would take nothing. Spike, observing Pawnee's refusal to eat, would not take food himself. It was as though he was going to let himself die if his best friend died. Only through the regaining strength of his friend would he regain his strength and live.

Once in awhile Spike would let out a whimper of agony and would reach over and lick Pawnee's forehead as he used to do so commonly when they frolicked and played together. It was a heartbreaking sight for the whole family. Pawnee did get weaker as Mom predicted, much weaker.

I can remember Mom taking us children into her bedroom and telling us that we had better try to prepare for the worst because she felt that Pawnee was not strong enough to pull through. We all cried and could not imagine what it would be like to lose Pawnee and possibly Spike.

On the fourth day something happened that put new life into all our hearts. Mom brought in a baby bottle filled with fresh cow's milk to try to feed Pawnee. Even if we had to force him to eat, Mom decided he had better get something into his stomach. As we entered the room, Spike was licking Pawnee's forehead again. At that moment, Pawnee slowly raised his head from the floor, reached out his tongue, and gently slid it across Spike's ear.

This gave us hope that he was going to make it. Pawnee took milk from the bottle, drinking like a baby. For the first time in four days, Spike took some food too, but only milk. It was as though he was telling us that he wanted nothing better for himself than his friend could eat. Pawnee and Spike use to eat from the same bowl, so this was Spike's way of saying to Pawnee that things were just like they used to be, and that everything was fine in their world again.

Everything was fine in their world again, or for the time being. Pawnee completely recovered and so did Spike. There was a patch on Pawnee's side that remained a scar because the hair did not grow back where the wound was. It was so large you could recognize Pawnee just by that patch from a great distance away.

I learned something from that experience that I will never forget. I learned what it was like to nearly lose your most dear pet. It instilled within my young mind the fact that someday I could lose him completely and never see him again. It was impossible in my world to have Pawnee forever. I wondered how I would react if the situation ever arrived for real and we lost him for good.

That summer we had a wonderful time with Pawnee and Spike. All the neighbors learned of our pet deer and all of them at one time or another asked us to bring Pawnee over for them to see. There was even a small article in a human-interest column printed in the

Bonners Ferry Herald town paper about Pawnee. We were all very proud of Pawnee and of course Spike.

That fall, during the hunting season we tied a red bandana around Pawnee's neck and locked him in the chicken pen when we were gone. The pen was a yard closed in by sparsely woven wire, was outdoors, and provided him protection during the deer-hunting season.

No incidents happened and we let Pawnee out right after hunting season ended. Pawnee had spent the winter with us. He and Spike slept in the enclosed porch of our home, keeping each other warm. There was not room for them both in Spike's doghouse, so this worked out fine for them both.

The next summer they could be seen romping through our clover and alfalfa fields again just like the previous year. It was refreshing to watch them for they represented nature in all her liveliness and splendor.

The day finally arrived that I dreaded the most. Mom received her second phone call from the Game Warden. This time it was bad tidings also. It seemed that Pawnee and Spike had been playing around one of our neighbor's homes and Pawnee had eaten the top of her freshly bloomed tulips clean off. She sent in a formal complaint to the Game Warden. It was his duty to keep such an incident from happening again.

The warden informed Mom that he would have to take Pawnee and put him on a game preserve. He said that he hated to do it, but he was forced to take action. He said that he would be out the very next morning to pick Pawnee up. He then asked her to lock Pawnee up so he would not wander off, and he would be there when he came by.

Of course this was a shocking blow to all of us, but according to Mom and Dad, there was nothing we could do. We put Pawnee in the barn across the road from our house. It was an old abandoned horse stable, and could be completely closed in by merely shutting the front doors. It was hard for us to lock him up as if he was a criminal or something.

The next morning when the Game Warden arrived, we all went out to the barn to hand over Pawnee. When we opened the door he was nowhere to be found. There was no obvious way that he could have escaped, because the doors and windows were all boarded over except for the main door which we had securely bolted shut.

Further investigation revealed a large opened trap door in the hayloft of the barn. This was used to pitch loose hay down to the horses below that were previously kept in the barn. Evidently, Pawnee had jumped a good twelve feet at an odd angle into the attic and made his escape through the hayloft outer door to freedom.

Pawnee remained hidden in the forest for the next three days. It was as if he had sensed danger and stayed away. On the fourth day he returned home just as if nothing had happened. Evidently he thought that everything was all right now, and the danger that had threatened him was gone.

Well, to his surprise and our dismay, it was not over. Mom made us put him back in the barn. We then nailed boards over the opening in the hayloft. The next day the Game Warden was back. He had a large burlap bag that he put Pawnee in and then heaved him into the back of his covered pickup truck. The way he treated Pawnee upset me and made me really mad.

I said, "You had better make sure that Pawnee gets a good home on a game preserve, or you will have to answer to me personally!"

The Game Warden looked at me with a frown as if to say, "Who do you think you are anyway? You can't doubt my judgment in this matter. I am the Game Warden! Not you!"

I rather surprised my Mom because I was usually timid and shy to strangers. I still could not believe completely that Pawnee was going to a game preserve. I could vision the warden taking him home and eating him. Venison is very good tasting meat, and Pawnee would have made him many delicious meals.

Spike was really upset over the whole situation. In fact, the Game Warden decided to leave rather quickly when Spike started growling and snapping his teeth at him. It was all we could do to hold him back.

"You had better get off our farm quick, or I'll turn Spike loose on you! I can not guarantee if I can pull him off you once he sinks his teeth in!" Joe exclaimed to the Warden.

Mom scolded us after the Warden left for acting so malicious towards him. She reminded us that he was just doing his job. Once our nearby neighbor had turned in her report he was bound by duty to do something. She also assured us that the Game Warden had promised her and Dad that he would indeed take Pawnee to the game preserve right there in our county. That, she said, would make him safe from hunters. He would also be able to grow up in the wilds of nature like he was meant to do.

Though I usually took everything Mom said point blank as absolute truth, for some reason I could not really believe that all this was true. I would have to have proof before I would believe this.

Shortly after this happened, Spike started refusing food again. He just moped around looking as if the world had come to an end for him. Just as we thought he might get sick from not eating, he disappeared and we never saw him again. It was quite a shock losing both Pawnee and our dog Spike in such a short time.

Our parents gave us another dog that we loved dearly, but no other pet ever set so dear in our hearts as much as those two had.

The wonderment of it all was we knew, or supposed we knew, that Pawnee was at the game preserve. That left the question, where was Spike?

It was four years later that the answer to several questions came to me. By then I was in the latter part of my high school training. I worked for the Idaho State Forestry during the summer months to earn enough money for school and clothing expenses.

We were sent up to a logging site near a game preserve in Boundary County to pile brush left by a licensed logger. State law required that they pay the State Forestry money to come in and clean up the mess they left while logging. This cleared the brush to help prevent forest fires and help the forest restore itself after the logging operations were finished in a particular area.

It was about ten o'clock in the morning when I threw down my axe I used to strip limbs from downed trees, and sat down on a stump for a cup of coffee and a sandwich. I had this strange feeling that something or someone was watching me. I looked up while sipping from my cup of coffee and noticed something across the small meadow from where I was working.

I saw a familiar sight. There standing and staring directly at me was a huge full-grown deer. I sensed something familiar about it, but I did not figure its true identity out until it slowly turned its side towards me and I could see a large scar on its belly. It was Pawnee! I felt goose bumps swell up on my arms, and I was elated at this site. Then I noticed a figure slowly coming out from the woods to join Pawnee, and believe it or not it was our lost dog Spike!

I could not believe my eyes. Spike had somehow traveled all that distance from our farm to this game preserve and found his forever friend Pawnee. This proved the limitlessness of instinct among animals. They had somehow weathered the past four years together. I could tell that their friendship was still as strong as ever.

I called to them, "Pawnee and Spike!"

Pawnee raised his head and turned it towards my voice as to signify that he indeed recognized me. Spikes ears perked up also showing familiarity of my voice. They would not approach me. I knew in my heart that they did know me. I could sense that, but for some reason they were afraid of me. It was as if they thought if they returned to me they would endanger their friendship again. I could see this and could understand their concern.

They must have stood there for five minutes more looking at me. I admired the huge rack of horns that adorned Pawnee's head. I then remembered how helpless he was when we found him along side his dead mother's body. He could surely take care of himself with those horns, I thought to myself. He could protect Spike also if he felt it was necessary.

I then heard Spike bark twice at me as if to say, "So-long old friend." Then they turned and darted off into the woods. I could see their free spirits had joined as one, and that they were truly one with Mother Nature again.

This scene restored my faith in many things. Nature in all her love and splendor had welcomed not only one of her natural children back into her arms of protection, but had made room for an outsider, our dog Spike.

After they left and I returned to my cup of coffee, thoughts of them raced through my mind. The good times I had with them. The memories of Pawnee's hook rug blanket Mom had made for him. How he would come into the house every afternoon at precisely 5:30 P.M. and lie down in front of the television on that rug and watch the "Art Linkletter Show," with his eyes glued to the set. Then he would get up and walk out the front door as soon as it was over.

I also remembered how Pawnee loved tobacco and would pull packs of cigarettes out of people's shirt pockets and eat them if they weren't quick enough to foil him. I remembered how he would sneak into the kitchen when Mom had her back turned and eat the butter right off the table.

I could not help thinking of the times I sat in the clover fields with Spike and Pawnee stretched out basking in the hot afternoon summer sun, while petting them as though they were two large puppies. I remember how special their friendship was to each other and to myself. I learned what a true friend was, seeing them watch over and protect each other all those years they were our pets. I also realized you don't really 'own' your pets. Their souls are free spirits just like ours. You may share a bond with them, but you can never own anything with such a soul as theirs, but just befriend and love them.

I was left with a feeling of loneliness and emptiness for the time being. But I was also left with many wonderful memories to cherish for all times. I swept the tears that were forming below my eyes from my face so the other guys on the crew would not see them. I sipped again from my coffee and . . . .

PEACE OF MIND

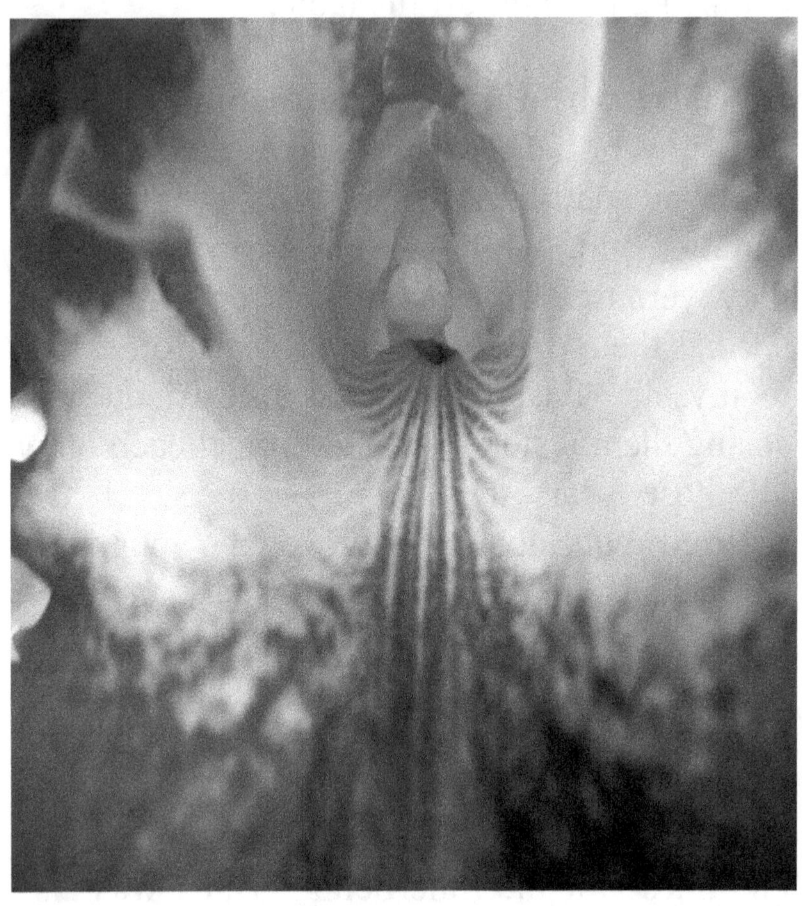

..........is feeling relaxed within yourself in your own little world. This makes you feel secure in your own realm. It will allow the strength, warmth, and love within you to shine into other people's worlds, causing a mutual sense of belonging as a world citizen, connected, yet somewhat separate from all.

Peace of mind is really undisturbed, you may cast a cloud around it so you cannot see or feel it as much but all you have to do is relax and it will appear. Even if all else seems in turmoil, your peace of mind is real.

INNER SECURITY

...........is an emotional and mental savings account that you have built up in your mind and soul throughout your years with warm feelings and precious memories of the good that has touched you in your life's journey.

The wonderful thing about such an account is that withdrawing from it does not deplete, but rather enhances and enriches it. So build up your inner security account. Fill it with fond memories and ease into them when you feel weak and draw strength from your inner past and self.

THE LITTLE BLANK BOOK

More than fifty years ago one of my friends gave me a little blank book. This friend told me that I should write my thoughts into that book because they so enjoyed my writings and my perceptions of life and emotions. They told me that I should write my life in that little blank book so I would never lose any of my insights into emotions, love, compassion, trust, faith, and the innocents of being.

I wrote in that little blank book over the years. I filled it up and many more just like it. When my life seems confusing and hard to comprehend, I reach into my bookcase, grab one of those little blank books, and read again those passages that I wrote from my experiences at various stages of my life. I am not speaking of a diary or chronological events, but rather perceptions of feelings, emotions, and how life touched me and I reflected it on those written pages.

Those little books give me great insight into myself. It is comprised of the values of love and life I had beginning at age eighteen. I was just out of high school and had recently moved from the simple life on a farm to the complexity of that of the big city of Seattle. It revealed the simplicity of my basic beliefs of love and life.

To my surprise my basic beliefs have remained unchanged over the years. In the last five decades many things have happened to me. I have suffered many hurts and many pains in that period of time. I have lived through the pains and heartbreak of relationships coming and going, suffered physical and emotional wounds in those fifty plus years, but my heart remained unchanged, my basic philosophy of love and life, emotional values, honesty, and faith have remained unchanged.

I am not saying these things to set myself up as a martyr, but rather to try to show you some insights into your own life. You must take precedence in the good that life has bestowed you and work for the betterment of today and your tomorrows, letting nothing stand in the way of your self-greatness.

Start Your Own Little Blank Book

I ask you to start your own little blank book. You can find them in almost any bookstore. They are bound just like any hard cover book you might find, but all the pages are blank. Use this little blank book as a sort of savings account of the good memories of your life. Feel free to spend time entering your past thoughts, hopes, goals, and wants, then write in it as life touches you from that point on.

Put in your feelings, your perceptions, your emotions, and your dreams. This will become a very powerful tool for enhancing your being because you will be formalizing your dreams by putting them in a goal-oriented format that will lead you towards their attainment.

The balance of this book contains a few of the thoughts and reflections that are from my very first little blank books starting fifty plus years ago. I hope they will add insight, hope, or pleasure as you read them and inspire thoughts, ideas, memories, goals, visions, hopes and prayers to fill the pages of your own little blank book.

REFLECTIONS

Excerpts from my Little Blank Books!

..........Your worth is the measure of the love you put forth.

..........The worlds of your mind are but a little hard work from the reality of your day.

..........I am going to clothe my soul with laughter and see it mature into a child - happily playing within my being.

..........There is nothing in this world that inner peace cannot overcome.

..........In this psychic world of ours, this forever changing and rearranging of life and land, the only feeling that will ride its way through the depths of eternity and show our grandeur on the other side is the little bit of love that we share this day.

..........Tension is just unchanneled love.

..........There is nothing in this world that can destroy the love I have. There is nothing in this world that can destroy the love I am.

..........Mankind seems to seek in love whatever he or she wants. Until they seek what they can give, it will evade them.

..........If you seek peace, do it in a gentle way. It is the simplicity of your convictions that harmonize your soul with nature.

..........Don't cry, just for today. The world is progressing through time and space and your cares are gently being left in the paths of destiny.

..........Love is joining hands and finding your souls have already touched.

..........Relax for a few minutes and think about your own reflections of how life has gently and lovingly touched you and those you love. Cherish those thoughts, as they will give you a glimpse into a better future for yourself and them.

..........Relax your troubled mind. Ponder maybe on a moment that might have been kind to you, but mostly look forward. Reach out from your pains, release your tensions to the wind, and let your cares flow down the streams in your mind. Live life in love like in your most precious dreams.

..........If you find peace but a moment at a time, cherish it, for that moment is the joy, the echo of mankind's destiny for all times.

..........Without a goal, life wanders through your universe creating nothing.

..........Peace is like the sun. It is always there in the space of your world even though during your dark hours you are unable or afraid to see it.

..........I found peace when I realized that I am not just for today. Therefore I don't need to prove my whole world or worth in the span of just twenty-four hours.

..........Today I met a new friend! I became aware of my own self.

..........As you are asleep, you attune your vision of life to that of the universe. While awake however, you shackle your destiny by forgetting your dreams and living by the guides of your consciousness.

..........Let tomorrow come with all its worries and problems, for I will never be a part of it. I am going to live my whole life right here within the comforting boundaries of today.

..........Choose wisely those that you let pass the threshold to your soul by your eyes, thoughts, hopes, and deeds.

..........Dream for peace and strive for bringing what you dream forward to touch other's hearts on your quest for the resolution of your soul and your interpretation of life.

..........Walk gently through life but leave only one imprint that if you had to walk that path again, or send your most cherished friend or loved one down to walk in it, you would do it with little or no hesitation.

..........Leave your own legacy! Each soul is unique and beautiful. Find what genius is in you and make it manifest. Create at least one foot print on your journey here that will proudly say you came this way and left an imprint of beauty; be it a song, a story, a poem, a smile, a child, or anything else of beauty.

..........Search in your heart whether you want to give away hate or love? If you could shed the weather of your choice upon yourself you must remember if that is sunshine, it may not be right for someone who loves walking in the rain and singing to the pouring clouds.

..........Never for a moment believe that all that is good to you should be put upon another. Let them find their own way to make their footprints on the sands of time.

..........We are all going forward in a new form of social evolution. If you seem stymied now then remember this pathway we call life is just one step on our long and wonderful journey. It leads us towards the finality of joining with all into a final consciousness of one! One life, One Soul, completely satisfied and filled with the realization that our quest for all the answers both simple and complex we sought were answered simply by one and only one word, Love!

A Moment Of Inner Peace

Let us reflect in **a moment of inner peace** to ease some of the stress from your dealings with our new normality of life for a while.

When life gets to be too hectic, serious, or hard to face, it is best to just relax and find a place of private solace to reflect on the beauty of nature to help calm your thoughts and soul. If you are unable to physically do that because of the various restrictions we are bound by in this day and age of Social Distancing, find a quiet place where you can be alone. Then close your eyes and run a scene such as this through your mind or a beautiful one from your own past memories.

"Down by the Lake"

Down by the lake I see ripples of water splashing against the shore pretending to be a wave from an ocean storm. Two ducks are bobbing their heads under the water forging for food.

The sun is shinning bright, earlier afternoon clouds have disappeared and the fresh after rain air fills my lungs.

A long walk to this place of solace, this piece of mind, was well worth the effort. I passed four leashed dogs all walking one man on my way here. Many cyclists are stretching their legs and pumping their bicycles along the road that winds with the curves of this beautiful lake.

A passing car or jogger running by while on their way to who knows where mutes the silence now and then. I see a woman casting a stick into the water and a huge black Lab jumping in to fetch it as though it was a valuable prize.

To the left my ears perceive the vocal cadence as a university rowing team steams their narrow little craft in front of me, their oars glistening in the sun as they churn the water again and again. They remind me of the wings of a series of humming birds or a line of dragonflies pushing their vehicle along at an unbelievable speed.

The thoughts of all of the woes of our modern world; the wars, the economy, the hunger, the sickness, the loneliness, and the strife suffered not only by the peoples of this great planet, but by its other animals, aquatic, and bird life, and the very breath of Mother Nature's atmosphere that we are so ignoring and polluting, fade away for these precious moments. My mind is calm, mimicking the glass smooth surface now returning to the lake as man, woman, dogs, and birds have drifted from my sight.

Ah! Such peace there is here. In a world of such strife and despair, there is this unfair haven of harmony tucked away from the world's cares and turmoil and I cherish this moment dearly.

One must frequently remove one's self from the busy and fast pace of life and experience the silence of mind, nature, and soul. Only by removing all thoughts and worries and heartaches from active play within ones mind can one truly speak to and speak from your heart and soul.

It is during the simplicity of no thought, no tense feelings, and no conscious assertion of will or ill will that you can really find a moment of inner peace.

A moment of inner peace can help you get through hours, days, weeks, months, and years of turmoil because you have to but relax your mind and return to that sacred moment of wellness of being and re-gather, refortify, ones hope, love, dreams, and goals in life.

"CASCADE de' COLOUR"

Photographed while backpacking in the North Cascades.
By: Jerry W. Miller

"Here I am, in the midst of nature, surrounded by the splendor of the forest. I hear the birds conveying their bliss to one another. I smell the fresh air of life as it emanates from all the foliage of nature.

My thoughts are taken back to my childhood where walks in the woods like this were a part of growing up. I feel the vigor of those days race through me, returning new insights into my reason for being.

As the sun breaks its way through the leaves revealing earth's rich ground, so does hope filter its meaning back into my very soul."

THIS YEAR

I will do my best to spread love this year whenever and wherever I get the opportunity.

Wherever I can plant a smile, I will do so.

If a burden can be lightened with a little of my love, so shall it be for my chief goal in life will be to share love.

If a kind word can be said to make another person feel enlightened, I shall say it.

If a touch of my hand on theirs can warm another's heart from the cold of living, I shall touch it.

If a blow can be stopped from causing pain to my brethren, I shall shield that friend with my life.

I am no martyr, but I realize that empathy is a means by which my life can have meaning rather than just wishes.

A COLD AND RAINY DAY
By: Jerry W. Miller

Give me a cold and rainy day
and I will show you love,

Reach your hand out from life's storm
and I will show you how.

It is not the storms of earth to fear,
but those you brew inside,

Nor the fires of the hearth that warm,
but the love you feel within.

To warm thy soul first, then thy flesh
gives reason to rejoice.

To share all this is more
than twice the love you would receive,

For nothing given is ever lost,
but those things kept hidden soon dissolve.

"Different Destinies
Same Universe!"
"Attack of the Giants
From Outer Space!"
"Teddy Bear!"
"Stealing from the Future!"
By: Jerry W. Miller

141

"Attack of the Giants From Outer Space!"

"A catastrophic view of Mankind's Destination, Evolution, or Destruction!"

"Attack of the Giants from Outer space" delves into the basic need for human kind to not only foresee, but take steps to prevent the impending destruction of our planet to the point that it will no longer sustain the human species or any other form of life as we know it today.

"Tebby Bear!"

"A Young boy's Journey to Manhood Across an Unwelcoming Universe!"

"Tebby Bear!" is a story about a young boy's journey to manhood after being purposefully sent across the universe to save his life from a catastrophic event happening on his home planet.

Thrust into the midst of our planet's physical, societal, ethical, and environmental parameters, he along with the help of his personal 'Tebby Bear' protection assistant, must find a way to survive, adapt, and grow to manhood while at the same time trying to find that elusive way back to his home planet and family.

"Stealing from the Future!"
"The price we pay may come due sooner than we think!"

"Stealing from the Future!" is a story about the harm that we are having upon our planet's environment while we continue denying any effects of Global Climate Change that are being caused by mankind!

Suppose the damage we inflict upon our future generations by ignoring our environment could cause us direct and immediate ramifications that were manifested before our very eyes! Perhaps then we would no longer deny that humans were the cause of our planet's atmospheric and environmental degradation, taking it from pristine to toxic!

This story takes a futuristic look at an age-old problem and the parameters necessary to change the minds and hearts of mankind before we inflict the final deathblows to our Mother Earth before it is to late!

Available in Paperback and Kindle @ Amazon.com

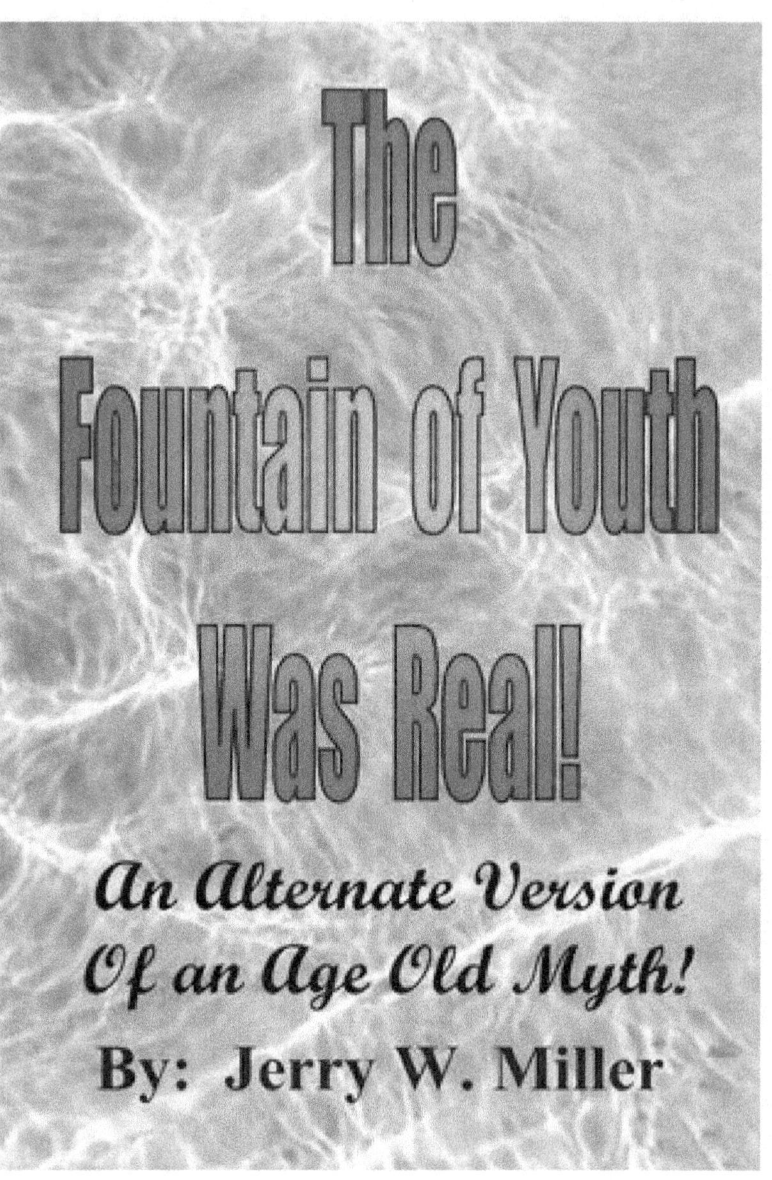

"The Fountain of Youth Was Real!"

An Alternate Version
Of an Age Old Myth!

History's accounts of certain events are sometimes changed for convenience, or shame, or pride, or just to save face. The official account of Ponce de León's pursuit of the Fountain of Youth, his failure to actually find it, and the intimate details of his death might have well been recorded in our history books conveniently skewed to create an alternate reality for nefarious reasons.

With that premise in mind let us follow another version of that all too familiar accounting of an illusive and intriguing search for a youth giving fountain. This time let us not just rely on the historians' version that centuries ago put quill pen and ink to parchment setting in stone their version of events. Rather lets hypothesize an alternate version of events from the other side of history, that being witnessed by the indigenous natives while suffering under the wrath, deceit, aggression, and lies of the so called conqueror Ponce de León!

Let us follow the path and journey of a young Indian brave from not only his youth to that of his manhood, but to the possibility of his discovery that could change forever our version of history regarding The Fountain of Youth and the historical recorded account of Ponce de León's demise.

Available in Paperback and Kindle
@ Amazon.com

Teach Me How to Read!

"A Journey into Literacy That Transcends Our Known Universe!"

By: Jerry W. Miller

This partial fantasy and partial realistic story takes place because of a strange and unworldly event that happened inside the local library in the small town of Bonners Ferry, Idaho. It transcends the bounds of earth and time in a unique way. It follows the plight of a young man who was saddled with many hardships including being illiterate, suffering from poverty, a severe stuttering problem, and the lack of a basic education. It follows his quest to overcome all of those obstacles especially his desire to be able to read, write, and communicate with others.

I think that you will find the parts of this story that are a bit on the fantasy side to be very intriguing. If nothing else, I hope reading this story will instill in you the importance of reading and possibly a new appetite to seek the mental experiences and knowledge you will attain from simply taking a break from your busy life and curling up with a good book.

Jerry W. Miller

Available in Paperback and Kindle @ Amazon.com

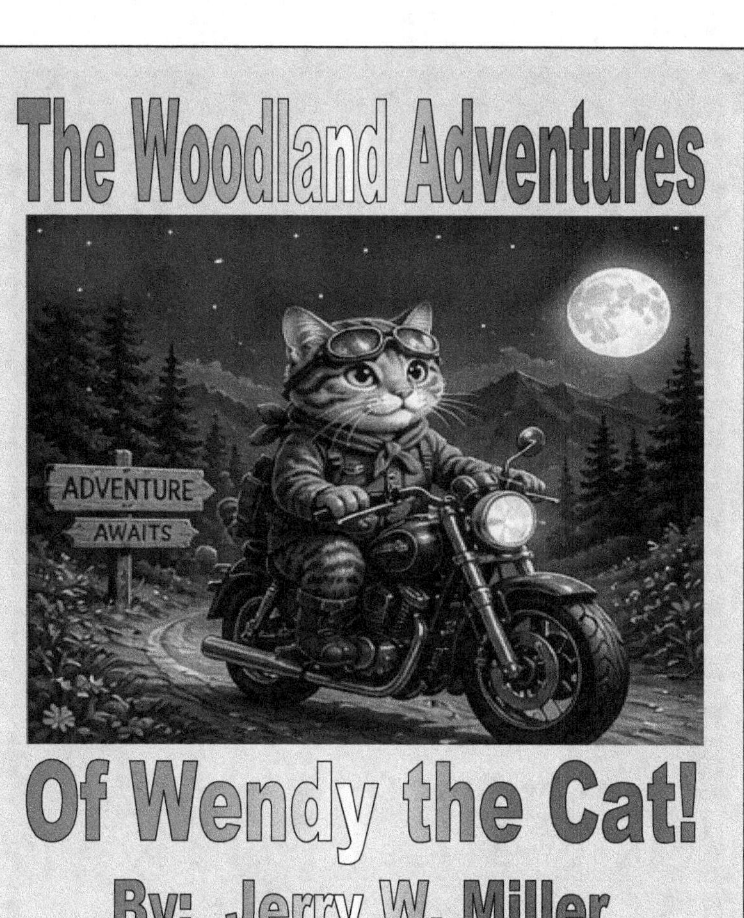

The Adventures of Wendy the Cat!" is a comical look at a make believe cat that loves taking adventures in the great outdoors. One can only imagine what adventures she will find fun and exciting to not only herself, but also those who read her stories!

"Pawnee & Spike Forever Friends" is a true story that took place on a country farm in North Idaho starting in or around 1958. I was raised in a family of sixteen children. We encountered quite a few things growing up but few compared to the heartwarming and amazing bond that grew between our border collie Spike and our pet deer named Pawnee!

www.ingramcontent.com/pod-product-compliance
Lightning Source LLC
Chambersburg PA
CBHW071511150726
48000CB00002B/535